discard

HORIZONS
Reading to Learn

Fast Track C–D
Textbook 2

Siegfried Engelmann

Susan Hanner

SRA McGraw-Hill

Columbus, Ohio

A Division of The McGraw·Hill Companies

Illustration Credits

Rick Cooley, Leslie Dunlap, Frank Ferri, Simon Galkin, Heidi King, Den Schofield, Jim Shough, Jessica Stanley.

SRA/McGraw-Hill

*A Division of The **McGraw·Hill** Companies*

Printed in the United States of America.

Send all inquiries to:
SRA/McGraw-Hill
250 Old Wilson Bridge Road, Suite 310
Worthington, OH 43085

ISBN 0-02-674216-0

1 2 3 4 5 6 7 8 9 VHJ 01 00 99 98 97

41

1	2	3	4
1. fronds	1. coconuts	1. <u>foot</u>prints	1. beyond
2. break	2. ankles	2. <u>out</u>come	2. stretching
3. echoed	3. dates	3. <u>rain</u>drops	3. edge
4. enough	4. bunches	4. <u>foot</u>ball	4. fluffy
5. bananas	5. trunks		5. ladder
6. juice	6. shelves		6. means

B Facts About Palm Trees

Today's story tells about palm trees.
Here are facts about palm trees:

- Palm trees grow in places that are very warm.
- Palm trees cannot live in places that get cold.
- Palm trees have very small roots.
- The branches of palm trees are called fronds.
- Some palm trees grow dates. Some palm trees grow coconuts.

fronds

coconuts

trunk

roots

Lesson 41 1

Bananas grow on plants that look something like palm trees. But banana plants are not trees.

C   Alone on an Island

Linda and Kathy walked along the beach. It was very dark, so they walked close to the waves. The waves washed up and swirled water around the girls' ankles. Then the waves fell back, pulling sand from under the girls' feet. Suddenly, Linda stepped into some very cold water, much colder than the water in the ocean. That cold water was running into the ocean. The girls were standing in a stream. Linda bent down and tasted the water. It was fresh water. "Kathy! Water!" she announced.

Kathy and Linda drank water until they couldn't drink any more.

Then they found a place near the palm trees where they could sleep. Linda didn't know how long she slept. But when she woke up it was morning. A strange sound woke her: "Caw chee, caw chee."

There were many large birds around the girls and many trees. Some trees were palm trees, with trunks that have shelves like a ladder. The birds were different colors. A few were white, many were red and yellow. Small black birds with yellow beaks made most of the noise. "I think those are myna birds," Linda said. "They're very smart."

"I'm hungry," Kathy said.

Linda stood up and looked around. She could see a beach of bright sand. She could see a blue sky and fluffy white clouds. She could see the ocean, stretching out until it met the sky. And she could see the crate, about twenty yards from the water. But she could not see a house, a boat, or any person other than her sister.

Linda and Kathy looked ⭐ around for something to eat. The girls found a plant that had large bunches of bananas growing on it. After the girls ate all the bananas they could eat, Linda said, "Let's walk down the beach and see if we can find out where we are."

"My feet hurt," Kathy said.

"We'll walk slowly," Linda said. So the girls started walking along the beach. They didn't go into the trees beyond the beach, because they were afraid that they would get lost. They walked and walked. They walked until the sun was high in the sky. Linda said, "It must be around noon time." But they did not see a house or a boat or any people.

They walked and walked until they came to a large rock. Linda climbed up on the rock and looked around. She saw footprints on the beach in front of her. The girls ran over to the footprints. Kathy said, "Other people are here. I see lots of footprints."

Linda looked at the footprints. She noticed a crate near the edge of the water. Linda said, "Those are our footprints. We have been walking in a circle. That means we're on an island. We walked all the way around the island."

Kathy started to cry.

Linda said, "Don't cry. Everything will be all right."

Linda didn't cry, but she felt like crying, too. She and her sister were all alone on an island. There was nothing on that island but trees and sand and a stream. How would they let anybody know where they were? How would they ever get off the island?

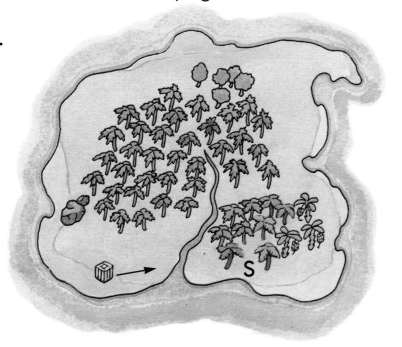

D Number your paper from 1 through 28.

1. Name 2 things that grow on different palm trees.
2. What part does the **A** show?
3. What part does the **B** show?
4. What part does the **C** show?
5. What part does the **D** show?

Skill Items

Here's a rule: **Birds have feathers.**

6. A crow is a bird. So what else do you know about a crow?
7. A bass is not a bird. So what else do you know about a bass?
8. A jay is a bird. So what else do you know about a jay?

Use the words in the box to write complete sentences.

billows	bunch	stretched	whirlpool	footprint
swirled	disappeared	enormous	outcome	

9. The smoke ___ in ___ ___.
10. The lifeboat ___ in the ___.

Review Items

11. What does ocean water taste like?
12. If you drank lots of ocean water, you would get ___.

Jar M is filled with fresh water. Jar P is filled with ocean water.

13. Which jar is heavier?
14. Which jar will freeze at 32 degrees?
15. Will the other jar freeze when it is **more than 32 degrees** or **less than 32 degrees?**

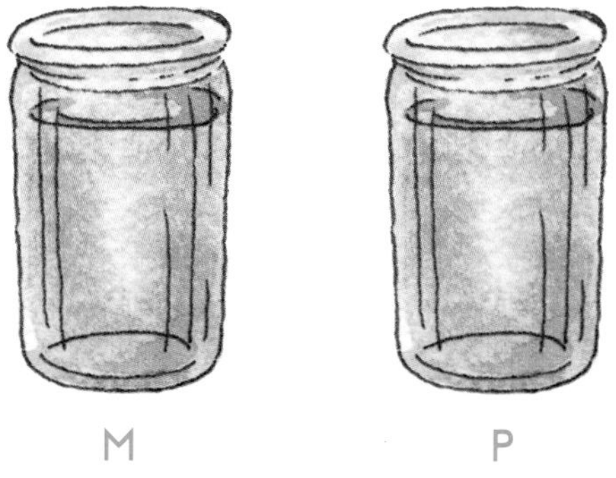

The ship in the picture is sinking. It is making currents as it sinks.

16. Write the letter of the object that will go down the whirlpool first.
17. Write the letter of the object that will go down the whirlpool next.
18. Write the letter of the object that will go down the whirlpool last.

19. When a plane flies from New York City to San Francisco, is it flying in the same direction or the opposite direction as the wind?
20. A mile is a little more than ▒▒▒▒ feet.

21. Write the letter of each island on the map.

22. **C** is not an island. Tell why.

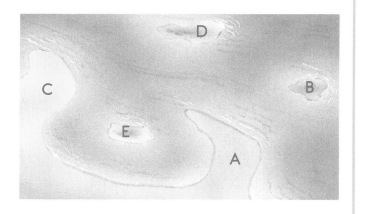

23. Write the letter of the animal that is facing into the wind.

24. Which direction is that animal facing?

25. So what's the name of that wind?

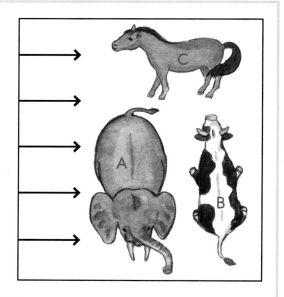

26. Let's say you are outside when the temperature is 40 degrees. What is the temperature inside your body?

27. Let's say a fly is outside when the temperature is 85 degrees. What is the temperature inside the fly's body?

28. Let's say you are outside when the temperature is 85 degrees. What is the temperature inside your body?

A

1	2	3
1. contest	1. echoed	1. monkeys
2. attach	2. explained	2. babies
3. though	3. screeched	3. shells
4. machine	4. peeled	4. raindrops
5. automobile	5. raised	

4	5
1. threw	1. hammer
2. outcome	2. inner
3. enough	3. foul
4. football	4. juice

B **Facts About** Coconuts

Here are facts about coconuts:
- A coconut is about as big as a football.
- Coconuts are not easy to open.
- Coconuts have two shells, one inside the other.
- Each shell is so hard that it wouldn't break if you hit it one time with a hammer.
- Inside the second shell is sweet, white coconut meat.
- Inside the coconut meat is sweet juice, called coconut milk.

The picture shows a coconut that is cut in half. The parts of the coconut are labeled.

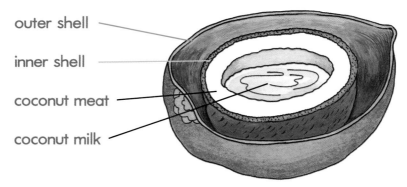

outer shell

inner shell

coconut meat

coconut milk

C Linda and Kathy Find More Food

Linda and Kathy were all alone on an island. Linda said, "Stop crying, Kathy. We are both very smart, and if we use our heads, we will get out of here."

Linda looked around and started to think. Then she pointed to the trees near the beach. "Those are coconut palm trees," she said to her sister. "Coconuts are good to eat. You can see them in the middle of the fronds," Linda pointed.

The girls ran to the trees and started looking under them. There were some coconuts on the ground, but they smelled foul and were covered with bugs. These coconuts were rotten. The girls kept looking. At last they found two good coconuts.

Kathy picked up one of the good coconuts and shook it. It sounded like a bottle that had water in it. Kathy said, "I'll

break it open." She threw it down on the sand as hard as she could. The coconut made a dent in the sand, but there was no mark on the coconut.

Kathy picked up the coconut and slammed it down in the sand again. But the outcome was the same.

"I don't know how to do this," Kathy said.

"I've got an idea," Linda said, and she explained her idea to Kathy.

The girls walked along the beach until they came to the large rock. It was almost six feet across. Linda climbed up on the rock and held the coconut in both hands. She raised her hands over her head, and she threw the coconut against the rock as hard as she could. Kwack—the sound of the coconut echoed. But there was no crack in the outer shell. After two more tries, the outer shell cracked open.

After the girls peeled off the outer shell,  Kathy said,

"Let me do it now." Kathy slammed the coconut against the rock four times before it cracked. Linda grabbed the cracked inner shell and held it so that not much juice leaked out. Then Linda carefully removed part of the shell. The girls ate all the coconut meat and shared the coconut milk.

"I'm still hungry," Linda said, "What about you?"

"Yes, me, too."

So the girls went to the banana plants and filled up on bananas.

Later, Linda said, "I'm tired of bananas. The trees are full of coconuts. We have to think of some way of getting them."

"We can't climb up there," Kathy said. "The trees are too tall and the coconuts are too high."

Linda pointed to monkeys in a tree and said, "I think I know how to get the monkeys to help us."

The girls walked along the beach until they came to a place where there were many monkeys in the trees. The monkeys were making a lot of noise. They were jumping and running through the trees.

"Let's make them mad," Linda said. Linda walked over to the trees. The mother monkeys picked up their babies and screeched at Linda. "Choo, choo, cha, cha, chee, chee, chee," they screeched.

Linda made a face and waved her arms at them. The monkeys got madder and madder. Linda went over to one of the trees and tried to shake it.

One of the monkeys picked a coconut and threw it down at Linda. Linda tried to shake the tree again. Another monkey threw a coconut at her. Other monkeys started to throw coconuts. Coconuts were coming down like raindrops.

Linda ran away from the trees. By now the ground was covered with fresh coconuts.

Kathy laughed. "We will have enough coconuts to last us for days and days," she said.

D **Number your paper from 1 through 25.**

1. How many shells does a coconut have?
2. Is it easy to break open a coconut?
3. What is the juice inside a coconut called?

The picture below shows a coconut that is cut in half.

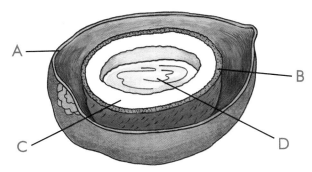

4. What part does the **A** show?
5. What part does the **B** show?
6. What part does the **C** show?
7. What part does the **D** show?
- inner shell
- fronds
- trunk
- coconut milk
- coconut meat
- coconuts
- outer shell
- dates
- roots

The picture below shows a coconut tree.

8. What part does the **A** show?
9. What part does the **B** show?
10. What part does the **C** show?
11. What part does the **D** show?
- inner shell
- fronds
- trunk
- coconut milk
- coconut meat
- coconuts
- outer shell
- dates
- roots

The occasional foul smell was normal.
12. What word means **once in a while?**
13. What word means **bad?**
14. What word means **usual?**

Look at objects A and B.
15. Write one way that tells how both objects are the same.
16. Write 2 ways that tell how object A is different from object B.

Object A   Object B

Review Items

17. Write **A, B, C,** or **D** to name the arrow that shows the way the cloud will move.
18. That wind is blowing from the ▨▨.
19. So that wind is called a ▨▨ wind.

San Francisco

20. Which eye works like one drop, a human's eye or a fly's eye?
21. Which eye works like many drops, a human's eye or a fly's eye?
22. Which eye can see more things at the same time, a human's eye or a fly's eye?

Some of the objects in the picture are insects, and some are spiders.

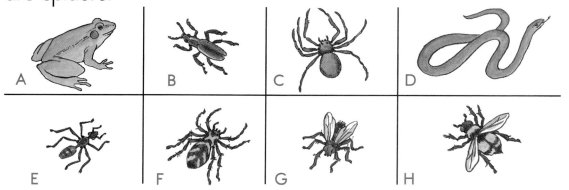

23. Write the letters of the spiders.
24. Write the letters of the insects.

25. Write the letters of the 9 places that are in the United States.

a. Denver
b. Turkey
c. Chicago
d. New York City
e. Texas
f. China
g. Alaska
h. Italy
i. Lake Michigan
j. California
k. San Francisco
l. Japan
m. Ohio

A

1
1. construct
2. force
3. steady
4. contest

2
1. jungle
2. rocky
3. silver
4. power
5. stronger

3
1. ledge
2. attached
3. though
4. haul
5. knives

4
1. raw
2. machine
3. vines
4. motor
5. automobile

B Facts About Machines

Some machines have engines or motors. A washing machine has a motor. An automobile is a machine that has an engine. Drills and blenders and lawn mowers are machines.

Some machines are very simple. Here's the rule about all machines: **All machines make it easier for you to do work.**

Here's a long branch. It can help you move a rock that is far too heavy for you to move by yourself.

Here's another kind of machine.

The two people are having a contest. Each person is pushing and trying to turn the log. The arrows show that person A is trying to move the log in one direction. Person B is trying to move it in the opposite direction. Which person is bigger and stronger?

Even though person B is much smaller than person A, person B will win this contest. Person A is pushing on the log. Person B is pushing on a handle that is attached to the log. That handle is a simple machine. It gives person B a lot more power than person A.

Remember, a long stick or a handle can be used as a simple machine. It gives a person a lot of power.

C Making Tools

The only things Linda and Kathy ate for two days were coconut meat and bananas. On the third day Kathy said, "I'm tired of eating bananas and coconuts. I want to eat something else."

"Me, too," Linda said. "I think that we should catch some fish."

Kathy said, "Catch some fish? I'm not hungry enough to eat raw fish."

"Well," Linda said, "maybe we can figure out some way to cook the fish."

"Okay," Kathy said, "but I won't eat raw fish." Then she added, "How can we catch fish without any fishing poles or hooks?"

Linda said, "We can take the wooden crate apart and use the nails for hooks. We can take vines from the jungle and use them for lines."

So the girls took the wooden crate apart. They pulled the nails out and bent them by hitting them with rocks.

Then the girls found thin vines. They tied the vines to the nails. Linda said, "Now we need to put worms or bugs on our hooks."

They caught some big bugs and stuck them on the bent nails.

Linda and her sister walked to a rocky place on the beach. They put their lines in the water and waited. They waited and waited. They could see many fish in the water—big fish, little fish. Some fish were green with red marks around their heads. Some fish were long and silver, like knives cutting through the water. Once in a while, a dark form of a large fish would move through the light green water.

The girls could see the fish, but the fish did not go after the bugs on the hooks. The girls fished for almost two hours. Finally, Kathy caught a fish, but it was only about three inches long.

Kathy said, "We will never catch enough fish to have a fish dinner."

Linda said, "We have to think of another way to catch fish. Let's think."

The girls sat there on the sunny rocks and thought and thought. Finally Linda said, "I've got an idea. We will use a net. We will put the net in the water. When fish swim into the net, we will pull the net out of the water."

The girls went back into the jungle and got lots of vines. Then they tied the vines together. Soon they had a net. It was very heavy. Kathy and Linda could hardly haul it along the beach.

They finally hauled the net to a ledge of rocks over the water.

The girls dropped the net into the water and waited for fish to swim into it. Soon, there were many fish inside the net. Some of them looked nearly as big as Kathy.

"Let's pull the net up," Linda said. "Pull fast."

The girls tried to pull the net out of the water. But the fish were pulling the net in the opposite direction. The fish pulled the net farther into the water. "We're slipping!" Kathy cried. Splash! Both of the girls fell into the water.

As the girls climbed back onto the rocks, Linda said, "We'll have to think of a better way to pull the net out of the water."

D Number your paper from 1 through 25.

Use the words in the box to write complete sentences.

foul	swirled	echoed	normal	enough
billows	juice	enormous	inner	occasional

1. The smoke ▓▓ in ▓▓ ▓▓.
2. The ▓▓ ▓▓ smell was ▓▓.

Write words from the box that mean the same thing as the underlined parts of the sentences.

- the reason   • coconuts   • fronds   • echo
- crate   • finally   • the outcome   • frost

3. She was happy with <u>how things turned out</u>.
4. Many of the palm trees' <u>branches</u> broke off in the storm.
5. He filled the <u>wooden box</u> with dishes.

Review Items
Write **W** for **warm-blooded** animals and **C** for **cold-blooded** animals.

6. dog   8. pig   10. bee
7. cow   9. spider

The picture shows objects caught in a giant whirlpool.

11. Write the letter of the object that will go down the hole in the whirlpool first.

12. Write the letter of the object that will go down the hole in the whirlpool next.

13. Write the letter of the object that will go down the hole in the whirlpool last.

14. Palm trees cannot live in places that get ▬▬▬.

15. What are the branches of palm trees called?

16. Name 2 things that grow on different palm trees.

17. What part does the **H** show?
18. What part does the **G** show?
19. What part does the **E** show?
20. What part does the **F** show?

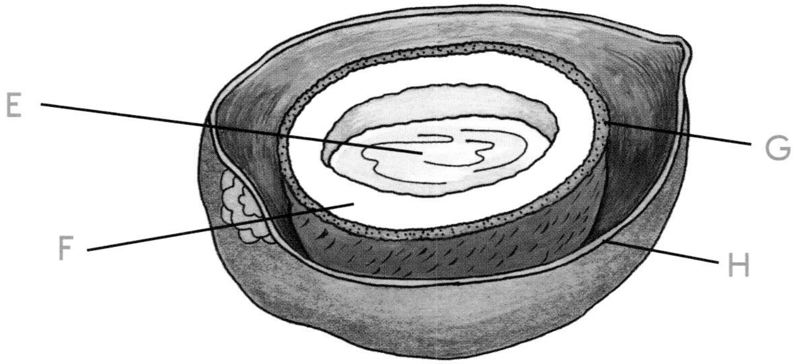

21. Lee is 8 miles high. Sam is 6 miles high. Who is colder?
22. Tell why.

23. The United States is not a state. It is a ____.
24. Japan is a ____.
25. The United States is made up of fifty ____.

A

1
1. imagine
2. neither
3. unpleasant
4. occasionally
5. shoulders

2
1. support
2. startled
3. seconds
4. gather

3
1. raw
2. force
3. burst
4. tied
5. twice

4
1. splashed
2. twigs
3. steady
4. construct
5. straightened

B

Linda and Kathy Construct a Machine

Linda and Kathy were not able to pull the net from the water when it was filled with fish.

Linda began to think of a way to solve this problem. She sat on the rocks near the edge of the ocean and thought. Waves rolled in and splashed against the rocks.

Suddenly, Linda jumped up and said, "I've got it."

Linda continued, "We will make a machine for pulling the net out of the water."

Kathy said, "I don't know what kind of machine that could be."

Linda said, "It's just a log with a long handle. We'll tie vines to the log. We'll turn the handle around and the vines will pull the net out of the water."

The girls found a small straight tree trunk. Then they got boards from the crate.

They pulled nails from the crate and straightened them by hitting them with flat rocks. Linda hit her fingers twice. That hurt.

Linda said, "Let's take a break." They sat on the rocks and watched the waves.

Suddenly Kathy pointed to something in the water and said, "Look. There's a white box."

Linda got a stick and pulled the box to shore. It had a big red cross on it. Linda said, "This is a first-aid kit. It must be from our ship."

The girls opened the kit and looked inside. Everything was dry. Kathy said, "Too bad it's not a box of things to eat."

"Look," Linda said and held up a small plastic box. Four matches were inside.

"Wow," Kathy said. "If those matches work, we'll be able to start a fire. Should we test one to see if it works?"

"No," Linda said. "There are only four of them. We may need all four to get a fire going."

Linda looked at her sore fingers and said, "I think we'd better get back to work." The girls went back to their machine.

Linda said, "Our next job is to use the boards from the crate to support the tree trunk."

An hour later, the girls had completed these supports.

PICTURE 1

Next, the sisters put the log in place and attached a handle to one end of the log. The handle was a board from the crate. They hammered three nails into it.

Now the machine looked like this:

PICTURE 2

Next, the sisters went into the jungle and found long vines. They tied them together and nailed one end of the vines to the log. They tied the other end to the net. Now their machine looked like this:

PICTURE 3

Linda explained, "We'll put the net out in the water and wait for fish to swim into it. Then we'll just turn the handle on our machine. The vines will wind around the log, and we'll pull the net up onto the beach."

So the girls waded out 🌟 into the water with their net. They went back up on the rock and waited. But no fish swam into the net. The day was hot and the wind was not blowing. The girls waited for more than an hour. Then a wind started to blow, and in a short time lots of fish started to gather close to the shore—some very large fish.

When there were lots of fish in the net, Linda said, "Okay, let's pull our net out of the water."

The girls ran up the beach to their machine. They grabbed the handle and turned it. It took a lot of force, but each time they turned the handle all the way around, the net got closer and closer to the shore.

PICTURE 4

The girls kept turning the handle. Linda's hands were sore, but she kept turning the handle and slowly, the net came out of the water. When the net was about 10 feet up the beach, the girls stopped turning and ran back to see what was in the net. It had lots of fish in it. Some of them were bigger than Kathy.

"Wow," Linda said.

Kathy said, "Let's put some of them back."

The girls kept four fish and put the rest back. The fish were glad to be back in the water, and they swam quickly from the shore.

Kathy said, "It's time to see if the matches work."

Linda said, "We'll need some dry grass and twigs." The girls found some and made a pile behind the rocks. Most of the time there was no wind here, but once in a while a hard gust of wind swirled through the grass and twigs.

The girls waited until the wind wasn't blowing. Quickly, Linda lit the first match and held it against the grass. Just then a gust of wind blew it out. The same thing happened to the second match. The third match worked. Within a few seconds, the whole pile of grass and twigs burst into flames.

"We did it," Linda said. "We're going to have a fish dinner."

C Number your paper from 1 through 26.

Skill Items

They constructed an enormous machine.

1. What word means **built**?
2. What word means **very large**?
3. What word names something that helps people do work?

Review Items

4. Let's say you are outside when the temperature is 40 degrees. What is the temperature inside your body?
5. Let's say you are outside when the temperature is 85 degrees. What is the temperature inside your body?
6. Let's say a fly is outside when the temperature is 85 degrees. What is the temperature inside the fly's body?
7. The stream water that Linda and Kathy found was different from the ocean water.
   Tell 2 ways it was different.
   The stream water was ▓▓▓ and ▓▓▓.
8. How many shells does a coconut have?
9. What is the juice inside a coconut called?
10. All machines make it easier for someone to ▓▓▓.
11. Name a state in the United States that is bigger than Italy.
12. Italy is shaped something like a ▓▓▓.

13. Write 2 letters that show bulkheads.
14. Write 2 letters that show decks.
15. Which letter shows where the bow is?
16. Which letter shows where the stern is?

17. Which arrow shows the way Linda's hand will move?
18. Which arrow shows the way the crate will move?

19. The biggest state in the United States is ▢.
20. The second biggest state in the United States is ▢.
21. A mile is a little more than ▢ feet.

22. Write the name of the state in the United States that is bigger than Japan.
- Ohio
- Alaska
- New York

23. You would have the least power if you pushed against one of the handles. Which handle is that?

24. Which handle would give you the most power?

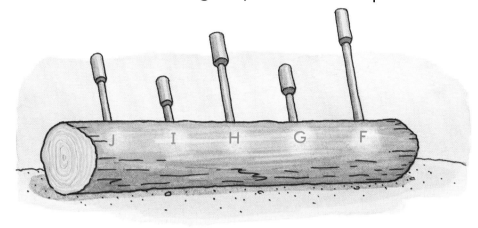

25. Write the letter of the plane that is in the warmest air.

26. Write the letter of the plane that is in the coldest air.

	5 miles high
D	4 miles high
G	3 miles high
F	2 miles high
	1 mile high

A

1	2	3	4
1. <u>after</u>noon	1. directly	1. buckle	1. gusts
2. <u>finger</u>nails	2. imagined	2. scales	2. settles
3. <u>over</u>head	3. crackling	3. unpleasant	3. turtle
4. <u>sea</u>shell	4. fading	4. neither	4. ugh
	5. nodded	5. orange	5. beauty
	6. scraped	6. task	6. foam

B # Figuring Out the Time of Day

Linda and Kathy do not have any clocks, so they cannot tell exactly what time it is. But they can figure out if it is morning, noon, afternoon, evening, or night. To figure out the time, they use facts about the sun.

Here are those facts:

- The sun always comes up in the east. That's called sunrise.
- The sun always goes down in the west. That's called sunset.
- When the sun is coming up in the east, it is morning.
- When the sun is right overhead, it is noon.
- When the sun sets in the west, it is evening.

The picture below shows the sun at different times of day. The arrows show which way the sun is moving.

West   East

Touch sun A. That is the first sun Linda and Kathy see in the morning. It is in the east.

Touch sun B. That sun is higher in the east. They see that sun later in the morning.

Touch sun C. That sun is right overhead. When they see this sun, they know it's around noon.

Touch sun D. That sun is moving down in the west. It is an afternoon sun.

Sun E is the last sun they see. That sun is in the west.

If you know where the sun is, you can figure out directions. If you face the sun that you see early in the morning, in which direction are you facing?

If you face the sun that you see at the end of the day, in which direction are you facing?

C The Girls Have Fish for Dinner

The girls had made a fire. Now there was a nice warm campfire burning on the ground a few yards from the stream.

Linda and Kathy had made the fire when the sun was almost directly overhead. They kept the fire going until late afternoon. They did that by putting sticks on it from time to time. The wind blew and the fire made crackling sounds. When the sun was setting in the west, the girls made the fire much bigger by putting some large dry branches on it. They needed a bigger fire to cook their dinner. Then the sisters began the unpleasant task of cleaning the fish.

"Ugh," Kathy said. "I don't want to do this."

"Me neither," Linda said. "But we've got to."

"I don't know how," Kathy said.

"We've got to scrape the scales off the outside of the fish. Then we have to take out the insides."

"Ugh," Kathy said. "I'll scrape the scales, but you'll have to do the insides."

"Okay," Linda said. Kathy used a seashell to scale the fish. She pressed a sharp end of the seashell against the fish and then scraped from the tail of the fish toward the head.

The scales popped off the fish. They were like little fingernails that you could see through. The scales stuck to everything. By the time Kathy had scaled two fish, her hair was covered with scales. So was her face. "Ugh," she said.

Linda made a knife from her belt buckle. She made the buckle sharp by rubbing it against a rock. She tied the buckle to a stick. She then used her knife to cut the fish open. She took out their insides and pulled out most of their bones.

• • •

There are very few places more beautiful than an island in the Pacific Ocean. And there are very few times of day more beautiful than sunset. The sun settles into the west, moving behind clouds that become filled with red and orange and yellow. The ocean looks dark, and the white foam and spray look gray in the fading light. The birds are quiet, and the breeze is sometimes warm and sometimes cool, as it gusts and stops and then gusts again.

That's how it was when Linda and Kathy ate their dinner that evening. They cooked their dinner in a large turtle shell that Kathy had found on the beach. They cooked some green plants with the fish. They drank fresh water and ate the fish and plants.

"This is about the most beautiful place in the world," Kathy said.

Linda nodded and looked out over the ocean toward the sunset. For a moment she felt the beauty of the sunset. Then she imagined that there were ships out there somewhere. Then she wondered how long it would be before one of those ships would find Kathy and her. Suddenly Linda felt cold and unhappy.

The picture shows the sun at different times of day.

1. Write the letter of the sun that shows when the girls made the fire.
2. Write the letter of the sun that shows when the girls finished dinner.
3. Write the letter of the sun you see early in the morning.
4. Write the letter of the sun you see at noon.
5. Write the letter of the sun you see at sunset.

Review Items

6. Linda and Kathy made a ▮▮▮ to help them pull the fish net from the water.
7. What did the girls use for a handle?
8. The girls hammered the handle to the end of ▮▮▮.

9. The girls got nails from .
10. They tied one end of the vine to the log and the other end of the vine to the ▓▓▓.
11. When the fish were in the net, how did the girls get the net out of the water?
12. Would it be easier to catch a fly on a hot day or a cold day?
13. Would a fly move faster or slower on a cold day?
14. A plane that flies from Italy to New York City goes in which direction?
15. Where are the gas tanks on a big jet?

16. What is the temperature of the water in each jar?
17. Write the letter of each jar that is filled with ocean water.
18. Jar B is not filled with ocean water. How do you know?

32 degrees	32 degrees	32 degrees	32 degrees	32 degrees	32 degrees
A	B	C	D	E	F

19. A mile is around ▓▓▓ feet.

Jar A is filled with fresh water. Jar B is filled with ocean water.

20. Which jar is heavier?
21. Which jar will freeze at 32 degrees?
22. Will the other jar freeze when it is **more than 32 degrees** or **less than 32 degrees?**

A   B

23. Write the letters of the 8 places that are in the United States.

a. Denver
b. Texas
c. Turkey
d. San Francisco
e. Ohio
f. Chicago

g. China
h. Italy
i. Lake Michigan
j. Japan
k. New York City
l. California

A

1
1. amazing
2. cough
3. notice
4. great
5. important
6. comparison

2
1. damage
2. edge
3. image
4. ledge
5. imagine
6. orange

3
1. <u>fore</u>head
2. <u>normal</u>
3. <u>signal</u>
4. <u>fifteen</u>th

4
1. chilled
2. shoulders
3. mumbled
4. occasionally
5. highest

5
1. fever
2. woven
3. built
4. waving
5. sliver
6. shaking

B **Facts About** Fevers

Your normal temperature is about 98 degrees. That's the temperature inside your body when you are healthy. Here are facts about fevers:

- When you have a fever, you are sick and your temperature goes up.

- Most fevers don't go over 101 degrees.
- A very high fever of more than 104 degrees may damage a person's brain.
- When people have high fevers, they may see things and hear things that are not real.

C Signaling for Help

Fourteen days had passed. Linda and Kathy were tired of fish and coconuts and bananas. They were waiting for a ship to come by. But for two weeks, no ship came.

Then on the fifteenth day Linda and Kathy heard something. It was an airplane. They ran out onto the beach and looked into the sky. Where was it?

They looked and listened for a long time. The sound of the plane got louder and louder, but still they couldn't see it. Then, all at once, it came over the trees. It was not very high. There it was, speeding over the beach.

The girls ran down the beach, waving their arms. They yelled, "Here we are. Here we are." They ran after the plane, but it went on, over the ocean. "Here we are. Here we are," they called.

They watched the plane get smaller and smaller. "Come back. Come back!" Kathy yelled. The girls watched the plane until they couldn't see it anymore.

"Maybe it will come back," Kathy said.

The girls looked at the sky for at least an hour. Then Kathy started to cry. "We'll never get off this island."

"Don't talk like that," Linda said. "We will get off this island. That plane didn't see us because we didn't give the plane much to see. So we'll make things that any plane or ship will see. We'll start right now by getting some rocks— lots of them."

The girls carried rock after rock onto the beach and put each rock in place. Soon the rocks formed the letters H-E-L. Linda and Kathy got more rocks. Now the rocks  formed H-E-L-P. The word was over 20 feet long.

When they had finished, Kathy said, "A plane should be able to see that."

Linda said, "Right, but a ship won't. We have to make another signal for ships."

The girls went to the highest hill in the jungle. They built a fire on the hill. Then they went back into the jungle to get lots and lots of green leaves.

Linda said, "We'll keep a big pile of leaves next to the fire. We'll keep the fire going all the time. When we see a ship, we'll dump the green leaves on the fire. The leaves will make a lot of smoke."

The girls kept the fire going for four days. On the fourth day, Kathy had a fever. Linda felt Kathy's forehead. It felt much hotter than a normal temperature. In fact, Linda thought that Kathy's temperature was over 101 degrees.

During the day Kathy slept on the hill near the fire. Occasionally, she woke up. Once, she mumbled something in her sleep about "the ship, the ship." The girls had woven some mats from leaves and vines. When the sun began to set in the west, Linda covered Kathy with one of these mats. She did that so Kathy wouldn't become too chilled by the cool air.

Just as the evening sky was turning bright yellow and orange, Kathy sat up. "A ship," she said. Her eyes were wide. She pointed to the south. "A ship. I see a ship."

"Take it easy," Linda said, putting her hands on Kathy's shoulders.

"No, no," Kathy shouted. "There's a ship." Her body was shaking.

Skill Items

Write the word from the box that means the same thing as the underlined part of each sentence.

supported	attached	jungle	contest
image	startled	rushed	fever

1. The <u>picture</u> was faded.
2. The gloves were <u>connected</u> to the jacket.
3. He was <u>suddenly surprised</u> by the loud noise.

Here's a rule: **Fish are cold-blooded.**

4. A whale is not cold-blooded. So what else do you know about a whale?
5. A shark is a fish. So what else do you know about a shark?
6. A snapper is a fish. So what else do you know about a snapper?

7. Look at object A and object B. Write one way that tells how both objects are the same. Write 2 ways that tell how object A is different from object B.

Object A   Object B

Use the words in the box to write complete sentences.

attached	constructed	occasional	steady
machine	normal	hauled	foul	force

8. The ▨ ▨ smell was ▨.
9. They ▨ an enormous ▨.

Review Items
10. How far is it from New York City to San Francisco?
    - 5 hundred miles
    - 25 hundred miles
    - 5 thousand miles
11. How far is it from San Francisco to Japan?
    - 5 hundred miles
    - 25 hundred miles
    - 5 thousand miles
12. What ocean do you cross to get from San Francisco to Japan?
13. How many legs does an insect have?
14. How many legs does a fly have?
15. How many legs does a bee have?
16. How many legs does a spider have?
17. How many parts does a spider's body have?
18. How many parts does a fly's body have?

19. Write the letter of the sun you see at noon.
20. Write the letter of the sun you see at sunset.
21. Write the letter of the sun you see early in the morning.
22. Write the letter of the sun that shows when Linda and Kathy finished dinner.

A

1
1. rescued
2. excited
3. lowered
4. survived
5. ordered
6. coughed

2
1. important
2. tugboat
3. newspaper
4. notice

3
1. S. S. Mason
2. S. S. Milton
3. dull
4. amazing
5. Reeves

4
1. sliver
2. fairly
3. reporters
4. harbor

B

Landing a Ship

Landing a ship is a lot like landing an airplane.

- Airplanes land in airports. Ships land in harbors.
- Airplanes load and unload at gates. Ships load and unload at docks.
- Sometimes a little truck pulls an airplane to the gate. Sometimes a little boat pulls a large ship to the dock.

The boat that pulls the ship is called a tugboat. The picture shows a tugboat pulling the S. S. Milton into a busy harbor in Japan. Another tugboat is helping turn the ship. Along the shore are many docks with ships parked at them.

C The Girls Are Rescued

Linda didn't really believe that there was a ship in sight. But she slowly turned her head and looked south. She saw dark water and more dark water and a sliver of white. It was a ship—a ship with the sun shining on one side of it. "A ship," Linda said out loud.

Kathy raised her arms and waved. "Hello," she hollered.

"They must be two miles away," Linda said. "They won't be able to hear us. We've got to make a smoke signal."

The girls dumped all the green leaves on the fire. After a few moments, large billows of smoke rolled into the air.

The sliver on the ocean seemed to be getting larger. "More smoke," Kathy hollered. The girls threw heaps of grass on the fire. The fire coughed out bigger and bigger billows.

The ship was an ocean liner like the one that Linda and Kathy had been on. Now Linda could see people standing on the deck.

"It's stopping!" Kathy yelled. "The ship is stopping!" Linda and her sister ran down the hill. Linda fell and cut her leg. But she didn't notice it. Linda got up and ran as fast as she could until she reached the shore. She waved her arms.

A little boat was slowly lowered down the side of the great ocean liner. The little boat started toward the shore. Linda was crying for the first time since the ship went down almost three weeks before. "We're going home," Linda said. "We're going home."

The boat came up to the beach. The girls ran into the ocean to meet the boat. One of the three men in the boat said, "I'm Captain Reeves from the ship S. S. Milton."

Linda said, "I'm ★ Linda Jones and this is my sister Kathy. We were on the ship S. S. Mason when it sank."

Linda looked at Kathy and smiled. Then she remembered something. "Kathy's sick," Linda said.

The captain felt Kathy's forehead and ordered the men in the boat to take her to the ship. Linda and the captain stayed on the island so that Linda could show how she and her sister survived for almost three weeks.

It was getting fairly dark when Linda showed the captain their simple machine. "Amazing," the captain said. Linda also showed the signal for airplanes that was on the beach.

"Amazing," the captain said again. "You're a very smart girl."

•   •   •

Linda felt very proud and very excited. Linda and her sister were stars on the S. S. Milton. Everybody wanted to talk to them and ask them questions or go swimming with them. The girls ate at the captain's table. Only very important people eat at the captain's table.

Kathy felt better the day after the girls left the island. The girls traveled on the S. S. Milton for one week. When a tugboat finally pulled the ship into the harbor at Japan, many small boats crowded around the S. S. Milton. The girls' father met them at the dock. There were newspaper reporters in the crowd, too. The reporters asked the girls many questions.

Then their father drove them to their new house in Japan. It was a very pretty house on a small hill with a large tree in the front yard. Linda's father said, "You've done so many things lately that you may find it dull living here."

Linda hugged her father. "No, Daddy, it won't be dull," she said. "I'm just glad to be here."

Kathy said, "Me, too."

D Number your paper from 1 through 17.

1. Airplanes land at airports. Ships land at ▓▓▓.
   • gates   • harbors   • airports
2. Airplanes are pulled by little trucks. Ships are pulled by little ▓▓▓.
3. Airplanes unload at gates. Ships unload at ▓▓▓.
   • gates   • docks   • harbors

She survived until she was rescued.
4. What word means **saved from danger?**
5. What word means **managed to stay alive?**

Review Items

6. Which object is the hottest?
7. What is the temperature of that object?
8. Which object is the coldest?
9. What is the temperature of that object?

A

20 degrees

B

60 degrees

C

35 degrees

10. Write the letter of every line that is one inch long.
11. Write the letter of every line that is one centimeter long.

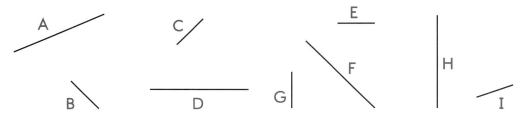

12. Palm trees cannot live in places that get ▬▬▬.
13. What are the branches of palm trees called?
14. Name 2 things that grow on different palm trees.
15. All machines make it easier for someone to ▬▬▬.

16. The arrow by the handle shows which way it turns.
    Which arrow shows the way the log moves?
17. Which arrow shows the way the vine moves?

━━━━━ END OF LESSON 47 INDEPENDENT WORK ━━━━━

SPECIAL PROJECT

Make a model of the machine that Linda and Kathy used to pull the fish net out of the water.

- For the tree trunk, use the cardboard tube from inside a roll of paper towels.
- For the handle, use a short pencil. Make a little hole in the tube and push the pencil through the hole.
- To hold the machine in place, use long pencils. Tie each pair of pencils together with rubber bands and stick the ends of the pencils in clay.
- For the vine, use string or make a thin vine from grass or other plants.
- For the net, use cheesecloth or make a net with string.
- For fish, make plastic cutouts or use small fish toys.

After you make your machine, you can show people how it works. Put the fish in a pan and fill the pan with water. Then put the net behind the fish and turn the handle to pull the fish from the water.

A

1	2
1. heart	1. future
2. touch	2. ago
3. bicycle	3. greater
4. fruit	4. tomorrow
	5. travelers
	6. yesterday

B   Comparing Things

When you compare two things, you tell how the things are the same. Then you tell how they are different. When you tell how they are different, you use the word **but.**

Look at object A and object B.

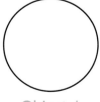

Object A   Object B

When you compare object A and object B, first you tell a way they are the same: **They're both circles.** Then you tell a way they are different: **Object A is big, but object B is not big.**

ιre object C and object D.
ι way they are the same.
a way they are different.

Object C

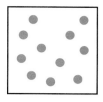

Object D

Compare object E and object F.
First tell a way they are the same.
Then tell a way they are different.

Object E

Object F

C Time Machines

In the next lesson, you'll read about a time machine.
There are no real time machines, but there are stories
about them. In these stories, the time machine takes
people into the future or the past. You could go back to
the year men first landed on the moon. Or you could go
to the year 2050. When time travelers go into the past,
they see how things were years ago. When they go into
the future, they see how things will be years from now.

In the story you will read, the people in the time
machine feel a great force as they go through time. A
force is a push. The greater the force, the harder the

push. If you put a book on top of your hand, your hand will feel the force of that book pushing down on your hand. If you pile ten books on your hand, your hand will feel much more force. If you were in the time machine that you will read about, you might feel the force of 500 books pushing against parts of your body.

D   Learning About a Time Line

You're going to read about some things that took place a long time ago and other things that will take place in the future.

The future is the time that has not happened yet. Tomorrow is part of the future. Next week is part of the future. Yesterday is not part of the future. It is part of the past.

What year is it now?

A year with a larger number is in the future. A year with a smaller number is in the past. The year 2300 is about 300 years in the future. The year 1700 is about 300 years in the past.

Let's say a girl was living in the year 1997. For her, the year 1996 would be in the past. For her, the year 1998 would be in the future.

Remember the rule about time: **The numbers for the years get smaller as you go back in the past.**

Look at time line 1. The word **now** is 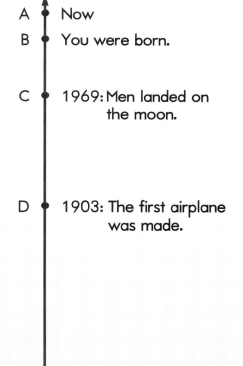 at the top of this time line.

The word **now** shows the time we live in right now. All the dots below **now** show times that are in the past.

Touch dot B on the time line. That dot shows when you were born. That dot is very close to the dot for now because you were born only a few years ago. What year goes at dot B?

Touch dot C. That dot shows when men landed on the moon. What year was that?

Touch dot D. That dot shows when the first airplane was made. What year was that?

Touch dot E. That dot shows the year the United States became a country. What year was that?

A • Now

B • You were born.

C • 1969: Men landed on the moon.

D • 1903: The first airplane was made.

E • 1776: The United States became a country.

TIME LINE 1

Time line 2 shows the future. The future is the part above the time it is **now**. On the time line, dot F is the year 2020.

What year is dot G?

Which is farther in the future, the year 2020 or the year 2320?

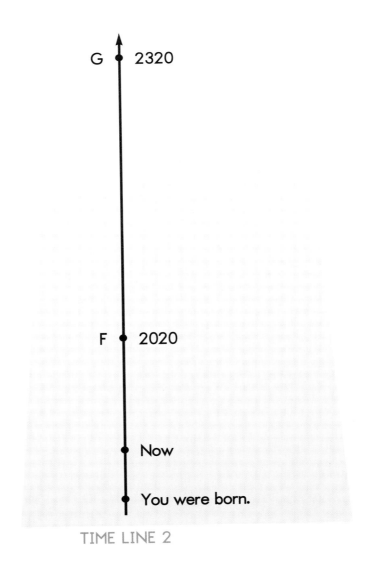

G • 2320

F • 2020

• Now

• You were born.

TIME LINE 2

E Number your paper from 1 through 27.

Look at object A and object B. Compare the objects.
1. Tell a way the objects are the same.
2. Tell a way the objects are different.

Object A

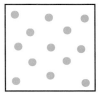

Object B

---

3. Are time machines **real** or **make-believe?**
4. A force is a ▇▇▇.

5. Which picture shows the largest force?
6. Which picture shows the smallest force?

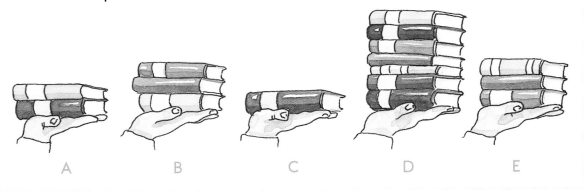

A   B   C   D   E

Review Items
7. Kathy's forehead was so hot because she had a ▇▇▇.

Lesson 48   **63**

8. How long were Linda and Kathy on the S. S. Milton?
9. Where did the S. S. Milton take them?

The ship in the picture is sinking. It is making currents as it sinks.

10. Write the letter of the object that will go down the whirlpool first.
11. Write the letter of the object that will go down the whirlpool next.
12. Write the letter of the object that will go down the whirlpool last.

13. Write the letter of each island on the map.
14. **D** is not an island. Tell why.

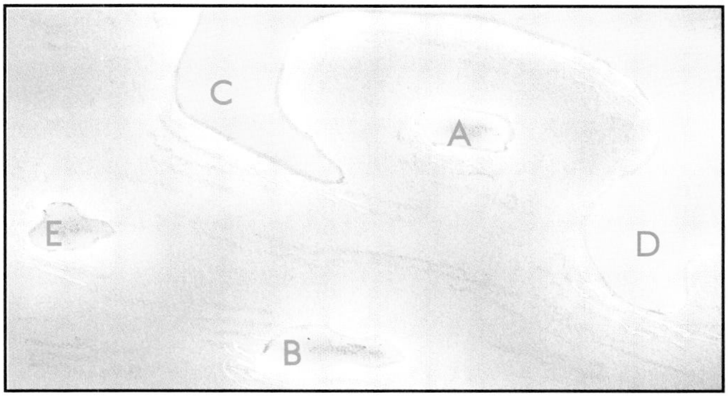

15. What part does the **J** show?
16. What part does the **K** show?
17. What part does the **L** show?
18. What part does the **M** show?

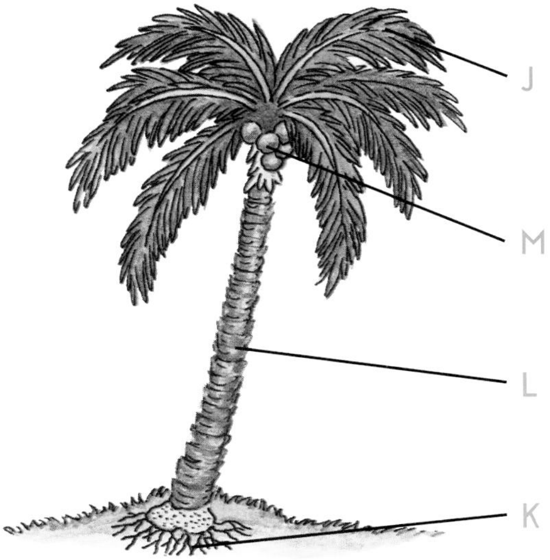

19. The temperature inside your body is about ____ degrees when you are healthy.
20. Most fevers don't go over ____ degrees.
21. Airplanes land at airports. Ships land at ____.
    - gates
    - airports
    - harbors
22. Airplanes are pulled by little trucks. Ships are pulled by ____.

23. Airplanes unload at gates. Ships unload at ____.
- gates
- docks
- harbors

24. You would have the least power if you pushed against one of the handles. Which handle is that?

25. Which handle would give you the most power?

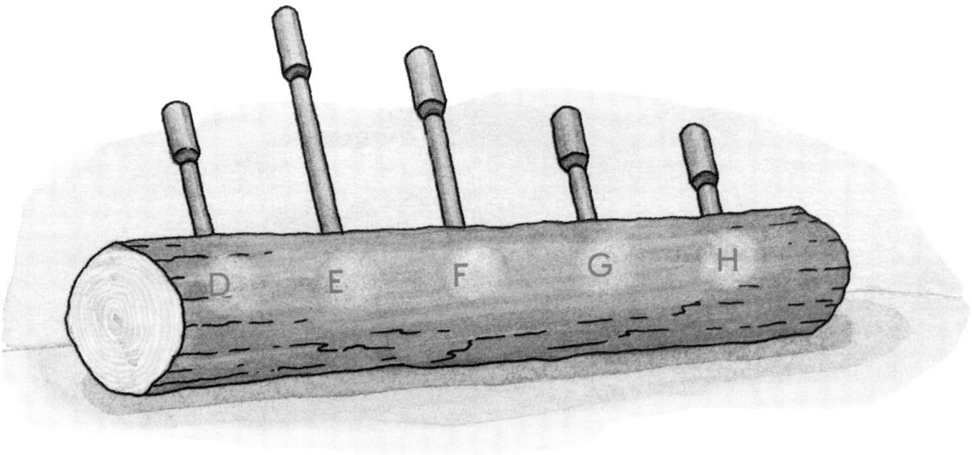

26. What is it called when the sun comes up?
- sunrise
- sunset

27. What is it called when the sun goes down?
- sunrise
- sunset

A

1	2
1. clicked	1. Thrig
2. dials	2. touch
3. flashing	3. heart
4. bicycles	4. fruit
	5. Eric

B Eric and Tom Find a Time Machine

Eric and Tom were with some other boys and girls. They had been at a picnic that was halfway up the mountain. Now they were walking home with the other boys and girls. As they walked down the mountain, they could see the town off in the distance.

Eric was tired. "Tom," he said, "let's rest."

Tom said, "I don't think that's a good idea. It's going to get dark pretty soon, and we might get lost."

"That's silly," Eric said. "All we have to do is follow the path. It goes right back to town. Are you scared?"

Tom said, "I'm not scared of anything."

It was very quiet up there on the side of the mountain— very quiet. The lights in the town were coming on. The other kids were far away by now. A cool breeze was blowing down the side of the mountain.

Then suddenly there was a loud sound. "Crrrrsssssk."
Tom jumped up. "Wh—what was that?"

Tom saw something flash through the sky.

It landed on the side of the mountain right above them. It looked like a metal pill. And it was as big as some of the trees on the mountain.

"Let's get out of here," Tom said. He grabbed Eric's arm, but Eric didn't move. He was standing there with his mouth open, looking at the pill.

Just then a door on the side of the thing opened, and an old man stepped out. He waved to Eric and Tom. "Hello," he called.

"Let's get out of here," Tom said again. Tom's heart was beating so hard that his shirt was shaking.

Eric waved to the old man. "Hello," Eric called, and started running toward the metal pill.

"Come back," Tom called. But Eric ran up to the old man. The old man was sitting on the ground. He did not look well. He was wearing a strange metal coat.

"Who are you?" Eric asked.

The old man said, "My name is Thrig."

Eric said, "Where do you live?"

Thrig said, "I live on Earth. But I live in a different time than you."

Tom and Eric looked at each other. Tom thought, "How can somebody live in a different time?"

Thrig then told Eric and Tom a very strange story. Thrig told them that he lived in the year 2400.

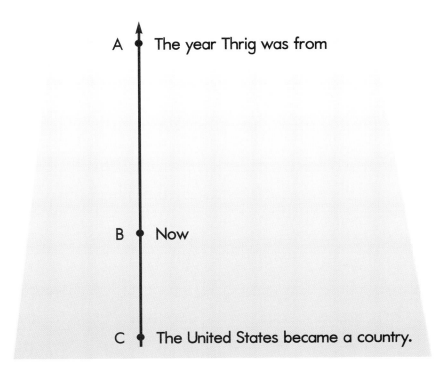

A The year Thrig was from

B Now

C The United States became a country.

Tom said, "The year 2400 will not be here for 4 hundred years. That year is 4 hundred years in the future."

Thrig nodded. "Yes, I live in the future," he said. He told the boys that he had made a time machine. This machine was the large metal pill. It could take him into the past or into the future. Thrig had just gone back in time 4 hundred years.

Thrig said, "But now I cannot go back to the year 2400," he said. "I am old. And when the machine goes through time, it puts a great force on a person's body. I do not think that I have enough strength to return to 2400." Thrig said, "I will spend the rest of my life here. I will never see my friends again."

Thrig looked very sad. "And now I must rest. The trip through time has made me very tired." Thrig closed his eyes.

"He's asleep," Eric said after a moment. Then Eric walked toward the time machine.

Tom grabbed his arm and said, "Let's get out of here before something happens."

Eric laughed. He said, "That time machine won't bite you." Eric pulled away and started toward the door of the giant machine.

Tom ran after Eric. He caught up just as Eric was going through the door.

The inside of the time machine was filled with dials and lights. There were red lights and green lights and orange lights. There were big dials and little dials. There were dials that buzzed and dials that clicked. "Let's get out of here," Tom said.

Eric walked over to a seat in the middle of the machine. He sat down. As soon as he sat down, the door closed. "Swwwwwshshshsh."

Eric grabbed one of the handles. "I wonder what this handle does."

"Don't touch it," Tom said. "Don't touch it."

Eric pulled the handle down a little bit. Suddenly more lights started going on. Dials started moving and clicking and buzzing. And then Tom felt a great force. He could feel it push against his face and his chest.

"We—we're going through time," Tom announced.

He heard Eric's voice. It sounded very far away. "Oh, no," Eric cried.

And then everything was quiet. The dials slowed down. Most of the lights stopped flashing.

Eric stood up and the door opened. The boys looked outside. For a long time they looked. They could not believe what they saw.

C Number your paper from 1 through 21.

Write the word from the box that means the same thing as the underlined part of each sentence.

• unpleasant	• direct	• except	• announced
• force	• imagined	• raw	• frisky

1. The path between their houses was <u>straight</u>.
2. The hot weather was <u>not very nice</u>.
3. Susan ate <u>uncooked</u> fish.

Here's a rule: **Insects do not have bones.**

4. A beetle is an insect. So what else do you know about a beetle?
5. A worm is not an insect. So what else do you know about a worm?
6. An ant is an insect. So what else do you know about an ant?

7. Compare object A and object B. Remember, first tell how they're the same. Then tell how they're different.

 Object A

 Object B

Use the words in the box to write complete sentences.

imagined	rescued	disappeared	machine
constructed	image	survived	twice

8. They ▨ an enormous ▨.
9. She ▨ until she was ▨.

Review Items

10. Which arrow shows the way the air will leave the jet engine?
11. Which arrow shows the way the jet will move?

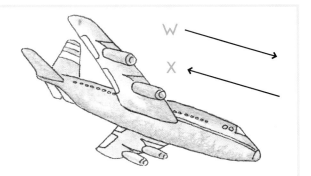

12. The biggest state in the United States is ▨.
13. The second biggest state in the United States is ▨.
14. Write the name of the state in the United States that is bigger than Japan.
    - Ohio
    - New York
    - Alaska

15. Write the letter of the plane that is in the warmest air.
16. Write the letter of the plane that is in the coldest air.

	5 miles high
Z	4 miles high
Y	3 miles high
X	2 miles high
W	1 mile high

17. Name a state in the United States that is bigger than Italy.
18. Italy is shaped something like a ▬▬.
19. A force is a ▬▬.

20. Which picture shows the largest force?
21. Which picture shows the smallest force?

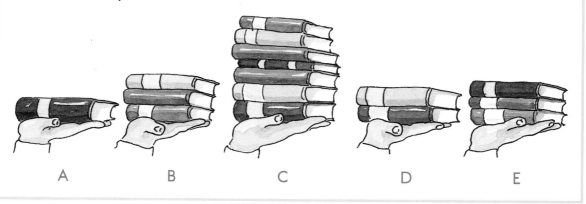

A   B   C   D   E

Number your paper from 1 through 36.

1. Palm trees cannot live in places that get ▮▮▮.
2. Name 2 things that grow on different palm trees.
3. All machines make it easier for someone to ▮▮▮.

4. You would have the most power if you pushed against one of the handles. Which handle is that?
5. Which handle would give you the least amount of power?

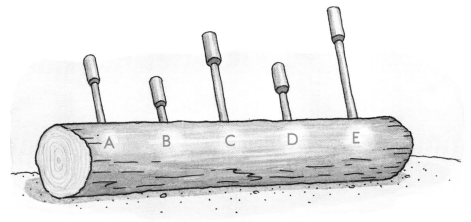

6. Airplanes land at airports. Ships land at ▮▮▮.
   • gates   • airports   • harbors
7. Airplanes are pulled by little trucks. Ships are pulled by ▮▮▮.
8. Airplanes unload at gates. Ships unload at ▮▮▮.
   • gates   • docks   • harbors

9. Write the letters that show tugboats.
10. Write 2 letters that show docks.

The arrow on the handle shows which way it turns.
11. Which arrow shows the way the log moves?
12. Which arrow shows the way the vine moves?

13. Write the letter of the sun you see at noon.
14. Write the letter of the sun you see early in the morning.
15. Write the letter of the sun you see at sunset.

16. The temperature inside your body is about ▆▆▆ degrees when you are healthy.
17. Most fevers don't go over ▆▆▆ degrees.
18. A force is a ▆▆▆.

19. Which picture shows the smallest force?
20. Which picture shows the largest force?

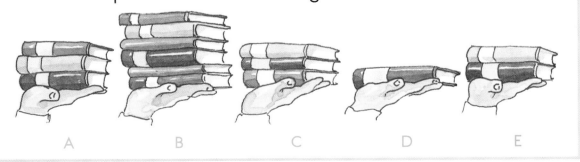

A   B   C   D   E

21. In what year did Eric and Tom find the time machine?

22. What year was Thrig from?
23. Is that year in the past or in the future?

24. What part does the **G** show?
25. What part does the **H** show?
26. What part does the **K** show?
27. What part does the **J** show?

Skill Items

Look at object A and object B. Compare the objects.
28. Tell a way the objects are the same.
29. Tell a way the objects are different.

Object A

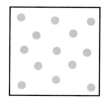

Object B

For each item, write the underlined word from the sentences in the box.

> The <u>occasional</u> <u>foul</u> smell was <u>normal</u>.
> They <u>constructed</u> an enormous <u>machine</u>.
> She <u>survived</u> until she was <u>rescued</u>.

30. What underlining means **built?**
31. What underlining means **saved from danger?**
32. What underlining means **usual?**
33. What underlining names something that helps people do work?
34. What underlining means **bad?**
35. What underlining means **once in a while?**
36. What underlining means **managed to stay alive?**

 END OF TEST 5

51

1	2	3	4
1. buried	1. <u>earth</u>quake	1. clomping	1. we'd
2. Egypt	2. <u>street</u>light	2. wider	2. center
3. palace	3. <u>news</u>paper	3. waking	3. hay
4. soldier	4. <u>tug</u>boat	4. bicycles	4. lean
5. pyramid		5. words	5. April
			6. fruit

B More About Time

In today's story, you'll find out what year Tom and Eric went to in the time machine.

That year was in the past, not in the future.

So you know that they did not go to some of the years below. Tell which years they did not go to.

a. 2450   b. 1880   c. 1900   d. 2600

Touch dot B on the time line. That is the year that Eric and Tom found the time machine. What year is that?

Touch dot A on the time line. That is the year that Thrig was from. What year is that?

Is that year in the past or in the future?

About how many years in the future?

Touch dot C. That is the year Tom and Eric went to. It is very close to the year the first airplane was made. What year was the first airplane made?

Did Tom and Eric go to a time that was **before** or **after** the first airplane?

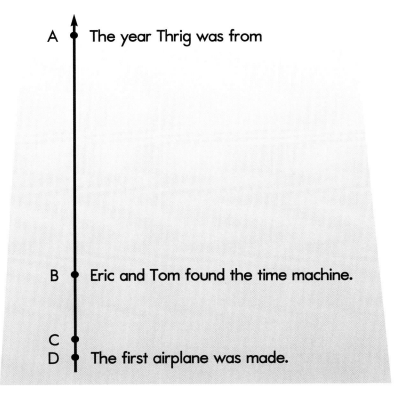

A — The year Thrig was from

B — Eric and Tom found the time machine.

C

D — The first airplane was made.

The San Francisco Earthquake

Tom and Eric looked out of the time machine. They were on the side of a mountain. Tom could see a large city in the distance. Lights were on all over the city, but they did not look very bright.

"Let's go down there," Eric said.

Tom said, "Remember, we don't know where we are. Let's be careful."

By the time the boys got to the city, the sky was very dark. The city had buildings and streets, but there was something strange about the city.

"I know what's funny," Tom said. "Most of the streets are made of dirt." Tom pointed to the streetlights. "Those are gas streetlights," he said. "Those are the kind of streetlights they had a long time ago."

Just then a clomping sound came down the street. The boys hid behind a fence. The sound came from a wagon that was pulled by a horse.

After the wagon went by, Tom said, "We've gone back in time, all right."

Eric said, "Things don't look very different."

Tom said, "You don't see any cars or trucks, do you?"

Then Tom said, "We'd better find a place to sleep."

They found a barn outside the city. They slept in the hay. Tom did not sleep very well. He had bad dreams.

Very early in the morning, the boys started to walk toward the center of the city. On the way they saw a newspaper in the street. They looked at the first page of the newspaper. The words that were at the top of the page said, "San Francisco Times."

Eric asked, "What's San Francisco?"

"San Francisco is a city," Tom said. "It is near the Pacific

Ocean." Tom looked at the date at the top of the newspaper: April 18, 1906.

Tom felt dizzy. He said, "We've  gone back in time about a hundred years." Just then Tom remembered that something happened in San Francisco in 1906, but he couldn't remember what.

Tom looked up. Three boys were standing in the street. They were wearing funny pants that stopped just below their knees. They were laughing at Tom and Eric. The tallest boy said to Tom, "You sure have funny clothes."

Tom looked at his clothes. They didn't look funny to him.

"Let's get out of here," Eric said. "Let's go downtown."

The boys walked past blocks and blocks of buildings. Some of the buildings were little and some were pretty big. But most of them were made of wood.

Most people were riding horses or they were riding in wagons pulled by horses. Some boys and girls rode bicycles. Tom and Eric saw only one car. It was one of the very first cars ever made. When the car went by, a horse went wild and started to run down the street. The horse was pulling a wagon full of fruit. Fruit spilled all over the street. Tom and Eric picked up some apples.

Just then, the street shook. The ground moved to one side. It moved so fast that Eric fell down. Then the ground moved the other way, and Tom could see a large crack starting to form right in the middle of the street.

Tom yelled, "I remember what happened in 1906. The earthquake! The San Francisco earthquake!"

Tom could hardly hear his own voice. People were screaming and running from buildings. A building on the corner started to lean and then it fell into the street. The crack in the middle of the street suddenly got wider and longer. The crack ran down the street. A horse and wagon slid and fell into the crack.

Suddenly, fires started to break out all along the crack. The crack had broken the gas lines, and now the gas was burning. Buildings were burning. The ground was shaking. People were running and screaming. Buildings were falling. "We've got to get out of here," Tom yelled.

Hundreds of men and women pushed this way and that way. The ground shook again. Another great crack formed in the street. It ran across the street and ran right between Eric and Tom. The crack got wider and wider. And suddenly Eric fell into the crack.

Review Items

1. Write the letters of the 4 names that tell about time.
2. Write the letters of the 4 names that tell about length or distance.
3. Write the letter of the one name that tells about temperature.
4. Write the letters of the 3 names that tell about speed.

   a. miles per hour
   b. miles
   c. hours
   d. meters
   e. centimeters per second
   f. weeks
   g. degrees
   h. minutes
   i. inches
   j. yards per minute
   k. years
   l. centimeters

The arrow on the handle shows which way it turns.
  5. Which arrow shows the way the log moves?
  6. Which arrow shows the way the vine moves?

  7. Write the letter of the sun you see early in the morning.
  8. Write the letter of the sun you see at sunset.
  9. Write the letter of the sun you see at noon.

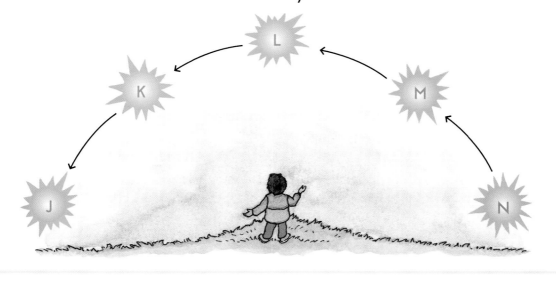

10. Airplanes land at airports. Ships land at ▩.
    - airports   • gates   • harbors
11. Airplanes are pulled by little trucks. Ships are pulled by ▩.
12. Airplanes unload at gates. Ships unload at ▩.
    - docks   • gates   • harbors

13. Which picture shows the smallest force?
14. Which picture shows the largest force?

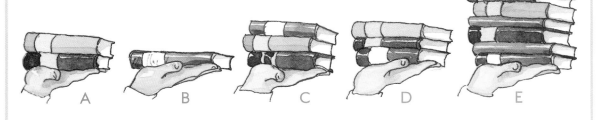

15. How many inches long is a yard?
16. About how many inches long is a meter?

Skill Item

17. Compare object A and object B. Remember, first tell how they're the same. Then tell how they're different.

Object A

Object B

A

1	2	3	4
1. guard	1. <u>fo</u>rever	1. slaves	1. blade
2. electric	2. <u>pa</u>lace	2. rafts	2. Nile
3. computer	3. <u>pock</u>et	3. queens	3. Egypt
4. appliance	4. <u>sol</u>dier	4. buried	4. sword
	5. <u>flash</u>light	5. recorder	5. pyramid

B More About Time

In today's story, you'll find out more about the trip that Eric and Tom took through time.

Touch dot B on the time line. That is the year Eric and Tom found the time machine.

Touch dot A. That's the year Thrig was from.

Touch dot C. That was the year Eric and Tom were in San Francisco.

You learned about things that were first made around the year 1900. Name those things.

A ● The year Thrig was from

B ● Eric and Tom found the time machine.

C ● Eric and Tom were in San Francisco.

C Facts About Egypt

The story that you will read today tells about Egypt.
Egypt is a country that is close to Italy.

Here are facts about Egypt:

- Egypt has a great river running through it. That river is named the Nile. Touch the Nile River on the map.

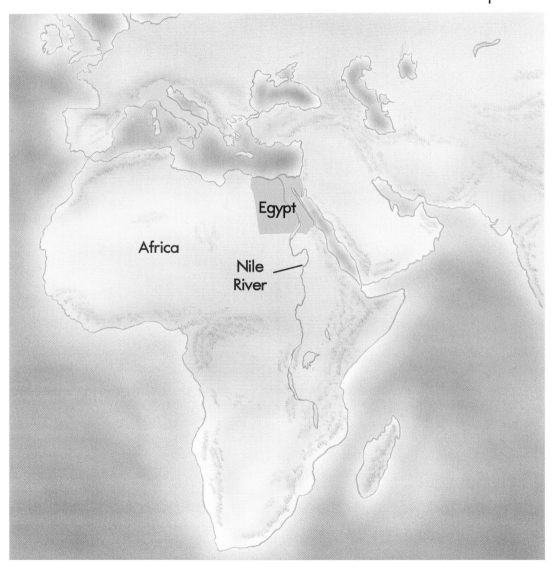

- Egypt is famous for its pyramids and palaces.
- Pyramids are huge stone buildings that are over five thousand years old. The picture shows pyramids.

- Dead kings and queens were made into mummies and buried in pyramids.

D **Eric and Tom in Egypt**

Eric had fallen into the crack in the ground. But Tom held on to Eric's hand. Tom looked down into the crack. It seemed to go down forever. Tom almost slipped. He pulled and pulled, and he finally pulled Eric out of the crack.

Then they ran. They pushed through crowds. From time to time, the earth would shake and knock them down. They ran past houses that were burning. They ran past houses that had fallen over.

When the boys got to the mountain outside the city, they looked back as they ran. The whole city was burning. They could hear people screaming in the distance. The boys ran up the side of the mountain to the time machine.

After they caught their breath, Tom said, "Let's figure out a way to get back to the right time."

They went inside the time machine. Dials were clicking and lights were flashing inside the machine. Tom sat down in the seat. The door shut: "Swwwshshsh." Tom pointed to the handle that Eric had pulled. "This makes the time machine work," Tom said.

Eric said, "When I pulled down on it, we went back in time."

Tom said, "I'll bet we will go forward in time if we push the handle up."

"Push it up," Eric said.

Tom grabbed the handle. It felt very cold. He tried to push it up, but it wouldn't move. "It's stuck," he said. "The handle won't move."

Eric pushed on the handle, but the outcome was the same.

"It's got to move," Tom said. He pushed and pulled with all his strength. Suddenly, the handle moved down. A force pushed against him.

Eric's voice sounded far away as he said, "Oh, no."

Lights went on and off. Dials clicked and buzzed. Then things began to quiet down. Eric said, "I'm afraid to look outside."

Tom stood up. The door opened. It was very bright outside. At first, Tom couldn't believe what he saw.

The time machine was on the side of a mountain above a great river. There were many rafts and boats on the river. But they did not look like any rafts and boats that Tom had ever seen before. Next to the river was a city. But it did not look like any city that Tom had ever seen before. All the buildings in the city were white. And next to the city were two great pyramids. One of them was already built and the other one was almost finished. Hundreds of men were dragging great stones toward this pyramid.

"We're in Egypt," Tom said. "We're in Egypt five thousand years ago! Look over there. The men are building a pyramid."

"What are pyramids for?" Eric asked.

Tom said, "When a king dies, they put him in a pyramid along with all of his slaves and his goats and everything else he owned."

Eric said, "Let's not leave the time machine now. We could take a nap. When it's dark, we'll go down to the city."

Tom and Eric slept. They woke up just as the sun was setting. Tom looked inside the time machine for a flashlight. He found one on a shelf. Next to it was a tiny tape recorder. He put the flashlight in one pocket and the tape recorder in the other.

Then Eric and Tom started down the mountain. They were very hungry. Down, down they went. They found a road at the bottom of the mountain. The road led into the city.

It was very quiet and very dark in the city. Tom took his flashlight out and was ready to turn it on when something happened.

E **Number your paper from 1 through 22.**

1. Some buildings in Egypt are over ▓▓▓ years old.
   - 7 thousand   • 15 thousand   • 5 thousand
2. What is the name of the great river that runs through Egypt?

3. Which letter shows where Italy is?
4. Which letter shows where Egypt is?
5. Which letter shows where the Nile River is?

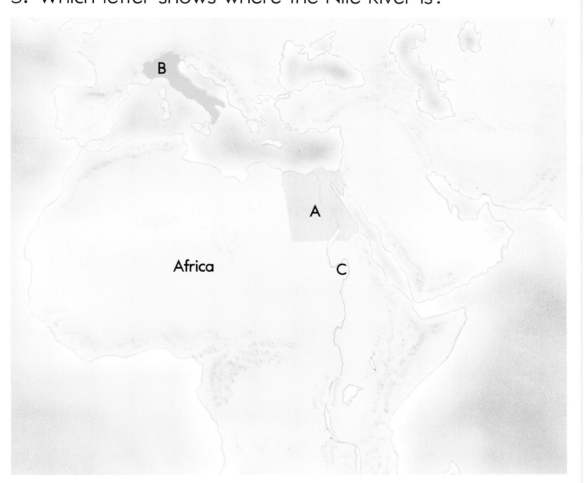

6. Compare object A and object B. Remember, first tell how they're the same. Then tell how they're different.

Object A

Object B

The palace guards spoke different languages.

7. What's the name of the place where a king and queen live?
8. What word refers to the words that people in a country use to say things?
9. What word names the people who protect the palace?

Review Items

10. Write the letters of the 9 places that are in the United States.

a. Italy   f. Denver   j. Texas
b. Ohio   g. San Francisco   k. Lake Michigan
c. China   h. Japan   l. Turkey
d. Chicago   i. California   m. New York City
e. Alaska

11. Write 3 years that are in the future.
12. What is it called when the sun comes up?
    - sunrise   - sunset
13. What is it called when the sun goes down?
    - sunrise   - sunset

14. You would have the least power if you pushed against one of the handles. Which handle is that?
15. Which handle would give you the most amount of power?

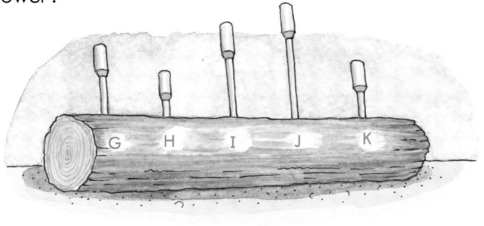

16. The temperature inside your body is about ▓▓▓ degrees when you are healthy.
17. Most fevers don't go over ▓▓▓ degrees.
18. Write the letters of the 4 years that are in the past.
    a. 1980   c. 2100   e. 1947
    b. 2010   d. 1897   f. 1994

19. Write the letters of the 4 names that tell about distance or length.
20. Write the letters of the 4 names that tell about time.
21. Write the letter of the one name that tells about temperature.
22. Write the letters of the 2 names that tell about speed.

a. weeks
b. minutes
c. hours
d. miles per hour
e. miles
f. centimeters
g. degrees
h. meters per week
i. years
j. inches
k. meters

A

1
1. radio
2. convinced
3. telephone
4. refrigerator

2
1. ton
2. bowed
3. lead
4. guard

3
1. wonderful
2. appliance
3. electric
4. computer

B   More About Time

Look at the time line.

Touch dot B. Dot B shows the year that Eric and Tom found the time machine. What year was that?

Touch dot A. Dot A shows the year that Thrig was from. What year was that?

Touch dot C. Dot C shows the year that Eric and Tom were in San Francisco. When was that?

Touch dot D. Dot D shows the year that the United States became a country. What year was that?

Touch dot E. Dot E shows when Eric and Tom were in Egypt. How long ago was that?

A ● The year Thrig was from

B ● Eric and Tom found the time machine.

C ● Eric and Tom were in San Francisco.

D ● The United States became a country.

E ● Eric and Tom were in Egypt.

C ▪ Reading Underlined Words

Sometimes you say some words louder than other words. One way to show the loud words is to underline them.

Here's what somebody said: "He thinks you are <u>wonderful</u>." When you say that sentence, you say one of the words louder than the others. Which word is that?

Say the sentence the way the person said it.

Here's what somebody else said: "<u>Maybe</u> they will get here on time." Say the sentence the way the person said it.

You will read stories that have underlined words. Remember to say them louder than the other words.

D ▪ Eric and Tom Meet the King of Egypt

Tom was ready to turn his flashlight on. Suddenly, a soldier was standing in front of him. The soldier had metal bands on his arms, and he held a large sword. He pointed the sword at Tom. "Ha hu ru," he said.

Tom looked at the soldier and said, "I don't know what you said."

The soldier moved the sword closer to Tom. Tom could see little marks on the blade. He could see a big scar on the soldier's hand. "Ha hu ru," the soldier said again.

Eric said, "He looks mad. We'd better do something."

The soldier yelled, "Ha hu ru," and shook his sword. But Tom still couldn't understand him.

The blade of the sword was only inches from Tom's face.

Tom put his hand over his face. He didn't remember that he had a flashlight in his hand. Without thinking, Tom turned it on.

When the soldier saw the light, he stepped back. He put his sword on the ground. "On kon urub," he said very softly. The soldier got down on his hands and knees. "On kon urub," he said again.

Eric said, "He thinks that you have some kind of great power. <u>Maybe</u> he thinks you are a <u>sun god</u>."

Tom smiled, "Maybe it will be fun to be a sun god."

Eric said, "Be careful, Tom."

Tom walked over to the soldier. "Take me to your <u>king</u>," he said. "The sun god wants to meet the king of Egypt." Tom pointed toward the middle of the city.

The soldier stood up. He bowed three times. Then he started to lead the boys down the streets. Soon they came to a large palace that ⭐ had hundreds of steps in front of it.

The soldier went up to three guards who were in front of the palace. The soldier talked and pointed to Tom. Then one guard walked up to the boys. The guard backed away and bowed three times.

Eric said, "I think he wants us to follow him."

So Tom and Eric followed the guard. Up the steps they went. Up, up, up to the great doors that led inside the palace.

"What a palace," Tom said. He had never been in a building so big. The hall seemed blocks and blocks long. And a soldier was standing every two yards on each side of the hall. There were hundreds of soldiers in that hall.

The guard walked down the hall. Tom and Eric followed. At last they walked through another huge door. They were now inside a great room looking at an old man. He was sitting on the floor with a large chain around his neck. At the end of the chain was a large metal ball. The ball looked like the sun.

The soldier said something to the old man. The old man looked at the boys for a long time. Then he smiled and stood up. He walked over and held out his hand. "Ura bustu," he said.

"He wants the flashlight," Eric said. "Don't give it to him."

"Don't worry," Tom said. Tom shook his head no. Then he pointed the flashlight at the sun on the old man's neck chain. Tom turned the flashlight on. The sun became bright.

The old man held his hand over the sun. "On kon urub," he said. "On kon urub."

Eric said, "Now <u>he</u> thinks that you're a sun god."

Skill Items

Write the words from the box that mean the same thing as the underlined parts of the sentences.

| train | a ton | hot | scale | mumbled |
| a pound | chilled | raft | degrees | |

1. They floated down the river on a <u>flat boat</u>.
2. The machine could lift <u>2 thousand pounds</u>.
3. She drank a glass of <u>cold</u> water.

4. Compare object A and object B. Remember, first tell how they're the same. Then tell how they're different.

Object A   Object B

Use the words in the box to write complete sentences.

| guards | amazing | languages | stretched |
| palace | future | rescued | flashed | survived |

5. She ▮▮▮ until she was ▮▮▮.
6. The ▮▮▮ ▮▮▮ spoke different ▮▮▮.

Review Items

7. Which letter shows where Italy is?
8. Which letter shows where China is?
9. Which letter shows where Turkey is?
10. Which letter shows where Japan is?
11. Is the United States shown on this map?

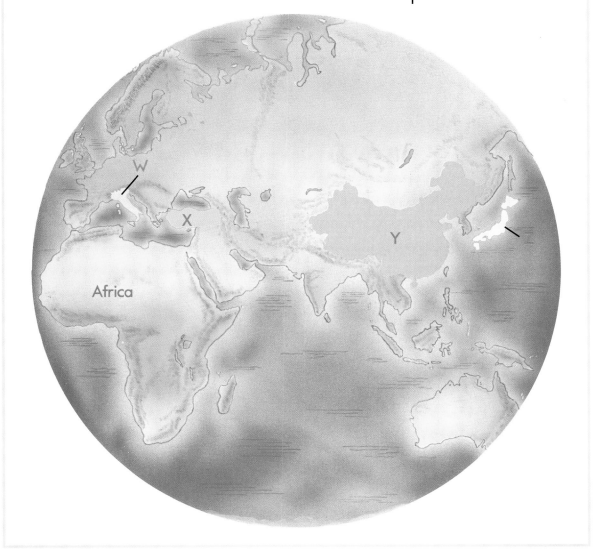

12. A plane that flies from Italy to New York City goes in which direction?

13. Some buildings in Egypt are over ▨ years old.
    - 20 thousand
    - 5 thousand
    - 8 thousand

14. When kings and queens of Egypt died, they were buried inside a ▨.

15. Write the letters of the 9 places that are in the United States.

    a. Denver
    b. Turkey
    c. Chicago
    d. China
    e. Alaska
    f. Italy
    g. Lake Michigan
    h. Japan
    i. New York City
    j. Texas
    k. San Francisco
    l. Ohio
    m. California
    n. Egypt

16. About how many inches long is a meter?

17. How many inches long is a yard?

18. A mile is a little more than ▨ feet.

19. Which letter shows Italy?
20. Which letter shows Egypt?
21. Which letter shows the Nile River?

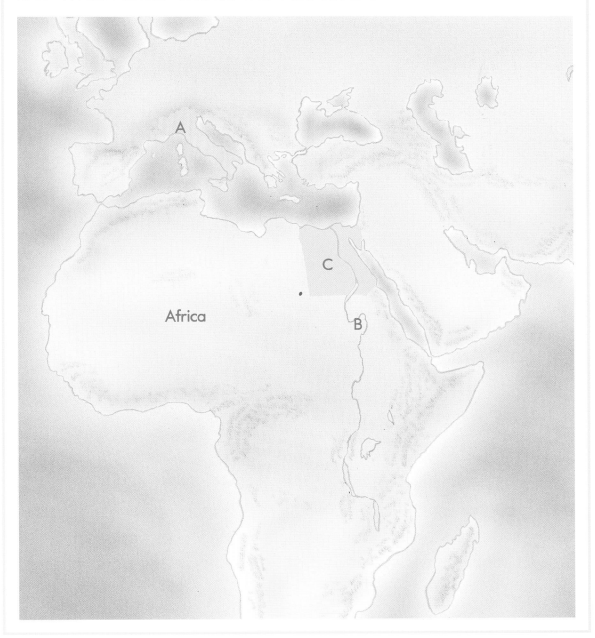

54

A

1
1. dishwasher
2. appliance
3. golden
4. insist
5. telephone
6. television

2
1. bulbs
2. radios
3. invention
4. refrigerators
5. computer

3
1. smashed
2. convinced
3. invented
4. snapped
5. pretended

4
1. throne
2. bowl
3. toaster
4. electric

B

Inventing

You live in a world that is filled with things that are made by humans. In this world are cars and airplanes and telephones and books. There are chairs and tables and stoves and dishes. There are thousands of things that you use every day.

Each of these things was <u>invented</u>. That means that somebody made the object for the first time. The person who made the first automobile invented the automobile. The person who made the first television invented the television. Remember, when somebody makes an object for the first time, the person invents that object. The object the person makes is called the invention. The first airplane was an invention. The first telephone was an invention.

Everything that is made by humans was invented by somebody. At one time, there were no cars, light bulbs, or glass windows. People didn't know how to make these things, because nobody had invented them yet.

Most of the things that you use every day were invented after the year 1800. Here are just some of the things that people did not have before 1800: trains, trucks, cars, airplanes, bicycles, telephones, radios, televisions, movies, tape recorders, computers, electric appliances like washing machines, toasters, refrigerators, or dishwashers.

C Eric and Tom Meet the King

Tom and Eric were in a huge palace. Tom had just convinced the old man with the golden sun that Tom was a sun god. The old man was holding his hand over the sun and saying, "On kon urub." Then the old man lifted the golden sun from around his neck and held it out for Tom. The old man bowed and said, "Ura, ura."

Eric said, "I think he wants you to have the golden sun."

Tom didn't want to take the sun, but the old man seemed to insist that he take it.

The sun was so heavy that Tom wondered how the old man could walk around with it hanging from his neck. Just as Tom put the chain around his neck, one of the guards handed him a pillow with a large gray cat sitting on it.

Eric said, "They think cats have special powers."

Tom felt silly with a large sun around his neck as he held a pillow with a gray cat on it.

Eric said, "I don't know about you, but I am very hungry."

Tom said, "Me, too." He handed the cat to the guard. Then he snapped his fingers. "Eat, eat," Tom said, and pretended to eat.

"Hem stroo," the soldier said smiling. "Hem stroo." The soldier ran from the room and down the hall.

Suddenly, many people came into the room. They were carrying all kinds of food. Tom looked at all of the food in front of him. He saw a large bowl. It had milk in it. Tom said, "I'll bet it's goat milk."

Eric tasted it. He made a face. "It's warm," he said. "Why don't they have cold milk?"

Tom said, "Their milk isn't cold because they don't have any way to keep it cold. Nobody had refrigerators until after the year 1800."

Tom and Eric ate and ate. Then the old man took Tom and Eric to their room. Tom put his flashlight in his pocket and went to sleep.

In the morning the old man took the boys to a great

room at the end of the hall. Inside the room a young man sat on a throne. The throne was made of gold and silver.

Eric said, "That young man must be the king."

"Hara uha <u>ho</u>," the king said. His voice was sharp.

Tom and Eric walked to the throne. The king stood up and walked to a window in the room. He pointed to the sunlight that was coming through the window. "Tasa u horu," he said. Then he pointed to Tom. "Umul hock a huck."

Tom knew what the king wanted. Tom pointed the flashlight at the king and pressed the button on the flashlight. But nothing happened. The flashlight did not go on. Tom pressed the button again. The outcome was the same.

"Aso uhuck," the king said. He snapped his fingers and two soldiers came forward. One of them grabbed Tom and the other grabbed Eric.

The king grabbed the flashlight from Tom's hand and threw it to the floor. It smashed. Tom looked at the flashlight. Then he looked up into the face of the king. The king looked very, very mean.

Skill Items

Write the word from the box that means the same thing as the underlined part of each sentence.

survived	damaged	lowered	rescued
woven	clomping	fixed	dull	center

1. Jane <u>saved</u> the child from the river.
2. Tom <u>broke</u> the bicycle when he ran over the rock.
3. She thinks that book is <u>boring</u>.

His argument convinced them to buy an appliance.

4. What word names a machine that's used around the house?
5. What word means he **made somebody believe something?**
6. What word refers to what he said to convince people?

Review Items

7. Airplanes land at airports. Ships land at ▒▒▒.
   • gates   • airports   • harbors
8. Airplanes are pulled by little trucks. Ships are pulled by ▒▒▒.
9. Airplanes unload at gates. Ships unload at ▒▒▒.
   • harbors   • docks   • gates

10. What is the temperature of the water in each jar?
11. Write the letter of each jar that is filled with ocean water.
12. Jar C is filled with ocean water. How do you know?

32 degrees   32 degrees   32 degrees   32 degrees   32 degrees   32 degrees

A   B   C   D   E   F

13. How many inches long is a yard?
14. About how many inches long is a meter?

15. In 1906, most of the streets in San Francisco were made of ▢.
    • bricks   • steel   • dirt
16. The streetlights were ▢. • not as bright • brighter
17. Most of the houses were made of ▢.
18. Write the letters of the 3 items that tell how people got from place to place.
    a. airplanes   c. wagons   e. trucks
    b. bikes   d. horses   f. buses
19. During the San Francisco earthquake, fires started when the ▢ lines broke.
20. What made the street crack?

21. Where did Eric and Tom go after leaving San Francisco?
22. In Egypt, how did Tom try to show he was a sun god?

A

1	2
1. ancient	1. Greece
2. language	2. spices
3. argue	3. grain
4. mammoth	4. further
5. saber-toothed	5. scratching

B

Greece

In today's story, you will read about the country of Greece. The map shows Greece as it is today.

Greece is a small country that is near Italy. It is north of Egypt. It is west of Turkey.

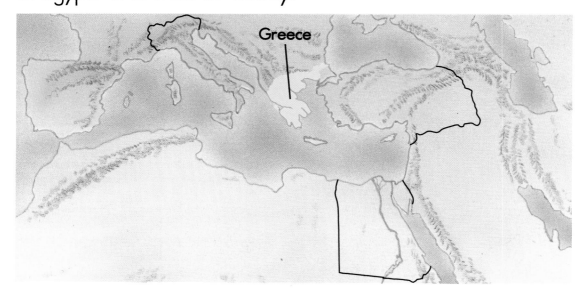

Greece

Eric and Tom Leave Egypt

A soldier was holding Tom. The flashlight was on the floor. It was broken. Tom could not play sun god anymore.

The king was yelling at the old man. Suddenly, Tom got an idea. He reached into his pocket and took out the tape recorder. He pressed the button. The king was saying, "Ra hu hub haki."

Tom held the tape recorder up high and played back what he had recorded. "Ra hu hub haki." The king stopped yelling. He looked at Tom. The soldier let go of Tom. Tom ran the tape back and played it again. He played it as loud as it would go. "Ra hu hub haki."

The king smiled and bowed. Tom walked up to the king. He pressed the button so that the tape recorder would record again. Then he said, "I am the sun god, and I have your words on this tape."

The king bowed and said, "Un uh, run duh."

Tom played the tape back as loud as he could.

Eric said, "Tom, let's get out of here before the tape recorder breaks. Remember what happened to the flashlight."

Eric and Tom walked down the long, long hall. They did not look back. They walked through the great doors of the palace. Then they started to run. They ran down the stairs—down, down. When they came to the bottom of the stairs, they kept on running. They ran down the streets of the city until they came to the river. Then they stopped.

They were both tired. People around them were pointing at them and talking, but Tom and Eric felt safe here.

Tom said, "That's the Nile River." He pointed to one of the huge rafts on the river. "That raft is carrying hundreds and hundreds of sacks of grain." Tom continued, "One raft can carry as much grain as a hundred wagons could carry."

"Why don't they use trucks?" Eric asked.

Tom laughed. "Nobody had trucks for thousands of years."

Eric looked at the rafts on the river. They carried all kinds of things—animals, furs, spices, food, and even great big stones the size of a car. "What are they going to do with those stones?" he asked.

Tom said, "They will use them to build a pyramid. They need thousands of stones to build one pyramid."

Just then a soldier came up to Eric and Tom. He held out his sword. "Ra uh hack stuck," he said.

Tom held up the tape recorder and played back the soldier's words. "Ra uh hack stuck." The soldier backed away.

Tom and Eric found a path that led up the mountain. They walked up and up. The mountain was very steep, and by the time they got to the time machine, they were tired and hungry.

They went inside the time machine. Tom sat down in the seat. "This time," he said, "I'm going to make the handle go up so we can go forward in time."

"I hope so," Eric said. "I don't want to go back any further in time."

Tom pushed up on the handle. It did not move. He moved in the seat. Then, suddenly, the handle moved up. Dials started to click and buzz. Lights went on and off. Tom felt the force against his face.

Then everything was quiet except for a few dials that were clicking and buzzing. Tom heard something scratching on the outside of the time machine. He stood up. The door opened. And something started to walk inside the time machine. It was a great big yellow lion.

D Number your paper from 1 through 22.

Write the years for
the things shown
on this time line.

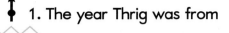

1. The year Thrig was from

2. Now
3. You were born.

4. Eric and Tom were in San Francisco.

5. The United States became a country.

6. Eric and Tom were in Egypt.

Skill Items

7. Compare object A and object B. Remember, first tell
how they're the same. Then tell how they're different.

Object A

Object B

Write the word from the box that means the same thing as the underlined part of each sentence.

ocean	always	pilot	attention	several
	although	globe	galley	whole

8. The plane's <u>kitchen</u> was very dirty.
9. He stayed home, <u>but</u> he wanted to go to the party.
10. She gave me <u>more than two</u> books to read.

Review Items

11. Write the letter that shows a tugboat.
12. Write 2 letters that show ships.
13. Write 2 letters that show docks.

14. In what year did Tom and Eric see the San Francisco earthquake?
15. When kings and queens of Egypt died, they were buried inside a ▨▨.
16. Some buildings in Egypt are over ▨▨ years old.
    - 5 thousand
    - 10 thousand
    - 15 thousand
17. When a person makes an object for the first time, the person ▨▨ the object.
18. Write the letter of each thing that was not invented by somebody.
    a. television   f. trains
    b. flowers   g. bushes
    c. grass   h. cows
    d. toasters   i. tables
    e. spiders   j. dogs
19. Most of the things that we use every day were invented after the year ▨▨.
    - 2000
    - 1900
    - 1800
20. What is it called when the sun goes down?
    - sunrise
    - sunset
21. What is it called when the sun comes up?
    - sunrise
    - sunset
22. Write the letter of each thing that was invented after 1800.
    a. dishwashers   e. buildings   i. rafts
    b. cars   f. computers   j. flashlights
    c. doors   g. hats   k. swords
    d. pyramids   h. chairs

A

1	2	3
1. <u>r</u>eplied	1. Troy	1. gift
2. <u>ar</u>gue	2. tame	2. Helen
3. <u>door</u>way	3. war	3. stared
4. <u>lan</u>guage	4. deal	4. ancient
5. <u>ar</u>my		

B

A Queen Named Helen

In today's story, you'll read about the country of Greece three thousand years ago. At that time, part of Greece was at war with Troy. The war began because a Greek queen named Helen ran away with a man from Troy. One thousand ships left Greece to go to war against Troy. The war lasted for ten years, but the Greek army could not get inside the walls around Troy.

The war ended when the soldiers from Greece tricked the army from Troy. The Greek soldiers built a large horse and pretended to leave it as a gift. Then the army pretended to leave. The soldiers from Troy took the great horse inside the walls of the city. Greek soldiers were hiding inside the horse. That night, they came out, opened the gates, and let the army from Greece inside the city.

C   Eric and Tom in Greece

A lion was in the doorway of the time machine. The lion was walking toward Tom. Tom could see the muscles in the lion's legs as it walked.

Suddenly, a man came through the doorway of the time machine. He was wearing a long white robe. He stared at the lights and dials. The man put his hand on the lion's back. The lion looked up at the man.

"That lion is tame," Eric said.

The man said something to Tom and Eric, but they could not understand the man's language. The man pointed toward the door of the time machine and then walked out of the time machine. Tom and Eric followed him.

The time machine was in a place that looked like a park. There were trees and grass. A few young men were standing and talking. Tom said, "I think we are in a school of long, long ago. I think we are in ancient Greece."

Eric said, "I thought we went forward in time."

Tom said, "Maybe we did, but not far enough."

The man in the robe said something and then pointed to a large table covered with food. "He wants us to eat," Tom said.

"Good deal," Eric said. "I'm really hungry. I don't even care if they give us warm milk."

After Tom and Eric ate, they watched the young men and their teacher. The teacher sat on a stone bench. The young men sat on the ground around him. The teacher asked questions. The young men would try to answer the questions. The teacher asked more questions.

Tom said, "I think they're learning how to argue. They argue so they can learn to think clearly. The teacher wants to show them that they don't know as much as they think they know."

"Why is he doing that?" Eric asked.

Tom replied, "So they will think about things."

Just then a man on a horse rode up. He stopped on the top of a hill near the school. ⭐ Then he called to the teacher. The teacher walked up the hill. Tom and Eric followed. Tom could see the ocean from the top of the hill. The man on the horse pointed to hundreds of ships on the ocean.

Tom and Eric looked at the ships. Eric said, "I have never seen so many ships in one place before. Where do you think they're going?"

Tom said, "I think we're in Greece three thousand years

ago. A queen of one city in Greece ran away with somebody from Troy." Tom continued. "So part of Greece went to war and sent a thousand ships into battle." Tom pointed to the ships below. "I think those are the ships that are going to Troy."

Some ships were loaded with soldiers and horses. Others carried large machines for throwing rocks through the air. Tom said, "Thousands of men will die in the battle with Troy. And that battle will go on for many years."

In the distance, Tom and Eric could hear the sounds of soldiers singing. Tom and Eric watched for a few minutes. The teacher standing next to them shook his head. He looked very sad.

"I think we'd better get out of here," Tom said. "I want to get back home."

Tom and Eric started to walk back to the time machine. The teacher and the young men were still on the hill.

Tom and Eric went inside the time machine. Tom sat down in the seat. The door closed. Then Tom said, "I wish I knew how to make this time machine work right."

Eric said, "Let me try. You didn't do very well the last time you tried."

Eric reached for the handle. Tom tried to push Eric's hand away, but Eric had a good grip on the handle. Suddenly, the handle moved down—almost all the way down. Before Tom could pull the handle back up, he felt the force against his face and ears.

"Oh, no!" Eric yelled. Then everything seemed to go dark.

D Number your paper from 1 through 24.

Write the time
for each event
on the time line.

1. The year Thrig was from

2. Now
3. You were born.

4. Eric and Tom were in San Francisco.

5. The United States became a country.

6. Greece and Troy went to war.

7. Eric and Tom were in Egypt.

Skill Items

Write the word from the box that means the same thing
as the underlined part of each sentence.

completely	steel	supposed	lowered
fish	boiled	moist	buried	tadpoles

8. She counted hundreds of <u>baby toads</u>.
9. His clothes were <u>slightly wet</u> from the rain.
10. Jan's bedroom was <u>totally</u> clean.

11. Compare object A and object B. Remember, first tell how they're the same. Then tell how they're different.

Object A   Object B

Use the words in the box to write complete sentences.

convinced	languages	modern	discovered	palace
argument	countries	dirty	guards	appliance

12. The ▨▨ ▨▨ spoke different ▨▨.
13. His ▨▨ ▨▨ them to buy an ▨▨.

Review Items

14. The temperature inside your body is about ▨▨ degrees when you are healthy.
15. Most fevers don't go over ▨▨ degrees.
16. A force is a ▨▨.
17. In Egypt, how did Tom try to show that he was a sun god?
18. When a person makes an object for the first time, the person ▨▨ the object.
19. In Egypt, Eric and Tom saw some huge stones on rafts. What were the stones for?

20. Why didn't the people in Egypt use trucks to haul things?

21. Which letter shows where Italy is?
22. Which letter shows where Egypt is?
23. Which letter shows where Greece is?
24. Which letter shows where Turkey is?

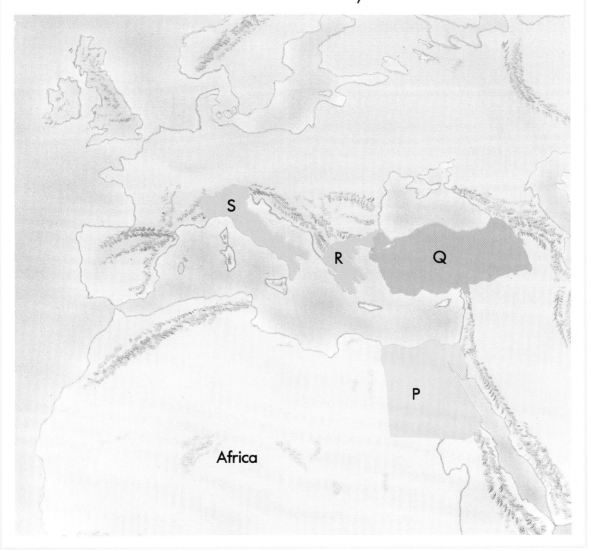

A

1
1. English
2. discover
3. future
4. brought

2
1. trumpeting
2. snorting
3. breathing
4. closing
5. crunching

3
1. tusks
2. charged
3. ponies
4. blinked

4
1. curved
2. tigers
3. spikes
4. Spain

B

Forty Thousand Years Ago

Things looked very different forty thousand years ago. There were no buildings or streets. The humans who lived then were a little different from the humans who live today. Some of them wore animal skins and lived in caves.

Many kinds of animals that you see today were around forty thousand years ago, but some of the animals from that time were different. The picture shows a saber-toothed tiger, a horse, a human, and a kind of elephant called a mammoth.

The saber-toothed tiger had a short tail and teeth like spikes.

The horse was much smaller than the horses of today.

The mammoth had long hair and long, curved tusks.

C Eric and Tom See Cave People

The force was so great that Tom's ears began ringing. He had trouble breathing. He couldn't talk. Then things inside the time machine looked brighter again. The dials and lights blinked and flashed.

"I hate to look outside," Eric said. His voice sounded funny.

Tom rubbed his eyes. "That handle went down almost all the way," Tom said.

Eric stood up and the door opened. The air was cool, and the trees outside looked a little different from any Tom had ever seen.

Eric and Tom stood outside the time machine for a few minutes. They looked in all directions, but they couldn't see any people. At first they didn't see any animals either. But then they heard a terrible roar.

A moment later, three very small horses charged down a hill. They were no bigger than ponies, but they looked different.

The horses ran through the long grass. Another animal was running behind them. It was very fast, but not as tall as the horses. Tom could see it leaping through the tall grass, but he couldn't get a good look at it. Suddenly, the horses turned and ran downhill. The animal that had been chasing them stopped and stood on top of a mound. Now Tom and Eric could see the animal clearly.

Eric said, "Do you see what I see?"

Tom didn't take his eyes from the animal. "Yes," he said.

The animal had a short tail, and two long teeth that stuck down like spikes. Tom said, "I think we've gone back about forty thousand years from our time. I think we're looking at a saber-toothed tiger."

Tom said, "Those other ⭐ animals were the kind of horses that lived forty thousand years ago."

Just as Eric started to say something, a loud snorting noise came from the other side of the time machine. The boys turned around. The animal making the noise was a

giant mammoth—an elephant with long fur and great tusks. It held its trunk high in the air. Its eyes were bright and it didn't look friendly. "Let's get out of here," Tom said. The boys ducked inside the time machine. Tom ran to the seat and sat down, but just as the door was closing, the mammoth charged into it. It made a terrible crunching sound. And the door wouldn't close. The door was open about a foot. The mammoth stuck its trunk through the open door and let out a great trumpeting sound.

The mammoth suddenly backed up and began to run. Some humans were running down the hill. The humans were dressed in animal skins. They were shouting as they ran.

The mammoth ran downhill. "Let's get out of here," Tom said.

The humans were coming closer to the time machine. They were about fifty yards away. They were shouting and growling. Tom had picked up a long branch. He was trying to bend the door so that it would close.

Two men were running toward the door. "Push on the door," Tom yelled. He was trying to bend the bottom of the door with the branch.

The men were only a few yards from the door now. Tom could smell them. "Push," Tom said. "Push."

"Blump." One of the men had thrown a rock and hit the side of the time machine. "Blump, blump, blump." More rocks.

One of the men grabbed the door. Tom could see his face and his teeth.

D **Number your paper from 1 through 27.**

Story Items

Here are the names of the animals you read about: **mammoth, saber-toothed tiger, horse.** Write the names of each animal.

1.   2.   3.

Write the time for each event on the time line.

4. The year Thrig was from

5. Now

6. You were born.

7. Eric and Tom were in San Francisco.

8. The United States became a country.

9. Greece and Troy went to war.

10. Eric and Tom were in Egypt.

11. Eric and Tom saw a saber-toothed tiger.

Review Items

12. Write the letters of the 2 years that are in the future.

 a. 1980   c. 1890   e. 2090
 b. 2140   d. 1750   f. 1990

13. Three thousand years ago, part of Greece went to war with ▮▮▮.
14. The war began because a queen from ▮▮▮ ran away with a man from Troy.
15. ▮▮▮ ships went to war with Troy.
    - 5 thousand
    - 1 thousand
    - 1 hundred
16. How long did the war last?
17. During the war, what kept the soldiers from getting inside Troy?
18. At last, the Greek army built a ▮▮▮.
19. What was inside this object?
20. What did the men do at night?
    - rang a bell
    - slept
    - opened the gate

21. Write the letter of the sun you see early in the morning.
22. Write the letter of the sun you see at sunset.
23. Write the letter of the sun you see at noon.

24. Write the letter of the one name that tells about temperature.
25. Write the letters of the 2 names that tell about speed.
26. Write the letters of the 4 names that tell about time.
27. Write the letters of the 4 names that tell about distance or length.

a. centimeters
b. minutes
c. years
d. inches
e. miles
f. weeks
g. degrees
h. yards per month
i. hours
j. miles per hour
k. meters

58

A

1	2
1. America	1. modern
2. Mexico	2. brought
3. Canada	3. future
4. Viking	4. languages
5. Columbus	5. discovered
	6. English

B **More About** Time

Look at the time line. Touch dot B. That dot shows when Eric and Tom started their trip. What year was that?

Touch dot A. That dot shows the year that Thrig was from. What year was that?

Touch dot C. That dot shows when Eric and Tom were in San Francisco. What year was that?

Touch dot D. That

A — The year Thrig was from

B — Eric and Tom found the time machine.

C — Eric and Tom were in San Francisco.

D — Eric and Tom were in Greece.

E — Eric and Tom were in Egypt.

F — Eric and Tom saw cave people.

dot shows when Eric and Tom were in Greece. How long ago was that?

Touch dot E. That dot shows when Eric and Tom were in Egypt. How long ago was that?

Touch dot F. That dot shows when Eric and Tom saw the cave people. How long ago was that?

C **Eric and Tom in the City of the Future**

"Push," Tom yelled. Just then a large rock hit the door. And suddenly the door closed. The rock must have straightened the door so that it could close again.

The door started to open again. "Quick," Tom said. "Sit in the chair so the door closes."

Eric ran to the seat and sat down. The door stayed closed now.

"Blump, blump." Rocks were hitting the side of the time machine.

"Push the handle up," Tom said. Eric bounced around in the seat and pushed on the handle. Rocks continued to hit the time machine.

Suddenly, the handle went up—far up. Tom almost fell down from the force. Then he almost passed out.

After a few moments, the force died down. Eric stood up, and the door opened.

The time machine was next to a huge building—the

tallest building that Tom had ever seen. There were buildings all around. Tom could not see the sun, only buildings. There were no streets and no cars—just buildings.

People were walking near the time machine. They wore funny clothes that seemed to shine.

Eric said, "We must have gone into the future."

A young man walked by the time machine. Tom said, "Can you help us?" The man looked at Tom and said, "Sellip." Then he walked away.

Tom and Eric stopped person after person. But every person said, "Sellip," and walked away. Finally, Tom stopped an old man. "Can you help us?" Tom asked.

The old man smiled. Very slowly he said, "I . . . will . . . try."

Tom and Eric grinned. Tom said, "Can you help us work our time machine?"

The old man made a face. Then he said, "Talk . . . slower."

Tom said, "Can . . . you . . . help . . . us . . . work . . . this . . . machine?"

The old man said, "No. We . . . have . . . machines . . . that ⭐ . . . fix . . . machines. People . . . do . . . not . . . fix machines."

Tom said, "Can . . . you . . . get . . . a machine . . . to help . . . us . . . work . . . our . . . time machine?"

The old man said, "That . . . time machine . . . is too old. We do not have . . . machines . . . that work . . . on such . . . old . . . time machines."

Tom felt sad. He and Eric would have to figure out how to work the machine by themselves.

The old man made a face. He thought for a few moments. Then he said, "What . . . year . . . are you . . . from?" Eric told him.

The old man thought and thought. "We . . . are . . . four thousand years . . . after your . . . time."

Eric said, "Why . . . do you speak . . . English? Nobody else . . . speaks . . . English."

The old man said, "I study . . . old, old languages. You . . . are very . . . lucky . . . to find me. No . . . other . . . people in the city . . . know . . . your language."

Eric asked, "What does . . . sellip . . . mean?"

The old man said, "Sellip . . . means this: I am . . . very sorry . . . that I cannot . . . help you. I . . . do not understand . . . your words. Good day."

Tom said, "Do you mean . . . that . . . one little . . . word . . . like sellip . . . means all that?"

"Yes," the old man said. "People . . . who live . . . in this time . . . do not have . . . to think . . . very much. So . . . the language . . . that they use . . . is very . . . simple. They . . . let the machines . . . do all . . . of their . . . thinking . . . for them.

Eric and Tom got into the time machine. Tom sat down and the door closed. Tom pulled the handle about halfway down. The dials buzzed. Lights went on and off. The force pushed against Tom's ears. Then it died down.

Tom stood up. The door opened. And outside the door, Tom could see water. On that water was a ship. But it wasn't a modern ship. It was an old-time sailing ship.

Number your paper from 1 through 25.

She survived until she was rescued.
1. What word means **saved from danger?**
2. What word means **managed to stay alive?**

Write the word from the box that means the same thing as the underlined part of each sentence.

humming	frost	frisky	rushing	announce
finally	humans	rusty	moments	

3. Many <u>people</u> were waiting for the train.
4. She watched the <u>playful</u> kittens at the pet shop.
5. The water was <u>moving fast</u> over the rocks.

Review Items
6. Write the letter of each thing that was invented after 1800.
   a. televisions
   b. cars
   c. doors
   d. telephones
   e. buildings
   f. computers
   g. hats
   h. chairs
   i. rafts
   j. flashlights
   k. swords

7. Three thousand years ago, part of Greece went to war with ▰▰.

8. The war began because a queen from ▰▰ ran away with a man from ▰▰.

9. ▰▰ ships went to war with Troy.
   - 10 thousand   - 1 thousand   - 1 hundred

10. How long did the war last?

11. During the war between part of Greece and Troy, what kept the soldiers from getting inside Troy?

12. At last, the Greek army built a ▰▰.

13. What was inside this object?

14. What did the men in that object do at night?

15. Write the letters of the 5 names that tell about time.

16. Write the letters of the 6 names that tell about distance or length.

17. Write the letter of the one name that tells about temperature.

18. Write the letters of the 3 names that tell about speed.

a. degrees	i. miles
b. minutes	j. meters
c. inches per year	k. feet per second
d. years	l. inches
e. miles per hour	m. feet
f. weeks	n. yards
g. centimeters	o. days
h. hours	

19. Write the letters of 3 things that were true of humans 40 thousand years ago.
    a. They were taller than people of today.
    b. They were shorter than people of today.
    c. They lived in caves.
    d. They wore hats.
    e. They wore animal skins.
    f. They rode bikes.
    g. They lived in buildings.
    h. They lived in pyramids.
    i. They drove cars.

20. Write the letters that tell about a mammoth.
21. Write the letters that tell about an elephant of today.
    a. short hair   c. long hair
    b. short tusks   d. long tusks

22. Write the letters that tell about a saber-toothed tiger.
23. Write the letters that tell about a tiger of today.
    a. short tail   c. long tail   e. long teeth
    b. no teeth   d. no ears   f. short teeth

24. During the San Francisco earthquake, fires started when the ▨▨▨ lines broke.
25. What made the street crack?

59

1	2
1. Mexico	1. Columbus
2. discovered	2. brought
3. America	3. Canada
4. angry	4. Vikings
5. countries	5. Spain

B More About Time

Look at the time line. Touch dot C. That dot shows when Eric and Tom started their trip. What year was that?

Touch dot A. That dot shows when Eric and Tom were in the city of the future. How far in the future was that?

Touch dot B. That dot shows the year that Thrig was from. What year was that?

A Eric and Tom were in the city of the future.

B The year Thrig was from

C Eric and Tom found the time machine.

D Eric and Tom were in San Francisco.

E Eric and Tom were in Greece.

F Eric and Tom were in Egypt.

G Eric and Tom saw cave people.

Touch dot D. That dot shows when Eric and Tom were in San Francisco. What year was that?

Touch dot E. That dot shows when Eric and Tom were in Greece. How long ago was that?

Touch dot F. That dot shows when Eric and Tom were in Egypt. How long ago was that?

Touch dot G. That dot shows when Eric and Tom saw the cave people. How long ago was that?

C # North America

In today's story, you will read about North America. Here are some countries that are in North America: Canada, the United States, and Mexico.

See if you can name all those countries that are in North America.

Touch each country on the map.

Remember, the United States is part of North America. But North America is bigger than the United States.

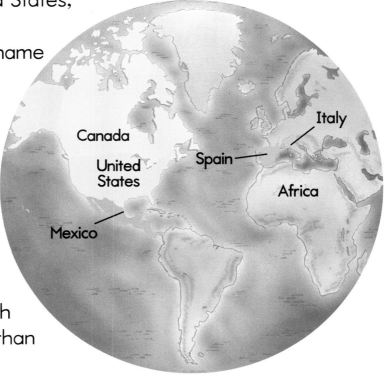

Canada
United States
Mexico
Spain
Italy
Africa

Spain in 1492

Tom and Eric were near an ocean. In the distance they could see an old-time sailing ship. There was a shack near the shore. Tom and Eric started down the hill toward the shack. A fat man standing next to the shack was wearing funny pants and a long cape. The man called out to Tom, but Tom couldn't understand what he said. Tom called, "Do you speak English?"

The man replied, "Yes."

Tom walked down to the shack. Eric followed him. Tom said, "What year is it?"

The man said, "1492."

Eric said, "Wasn't that the year that Columbus discovered America?"

"Yes," Tom said. "Columbus discovered America in 1492."

 The man became angry. "Did you say Columbus?" The man pointed to the ship at the dock. "That ship belongs to Columbus. Columbus is a crazy person."

The man went into his shack. Tom and Eric followed. On the walls were many maps, but they did not look like any maps that Tom and Eric had ever seen.

The man touched a spot on the largest map. "We are here in Spain. Columbus plans to sail his ships off the end of the world. He says that the world is round, but it is flat. If the world was round, we would roll off."

Eric said, "Everybody knows that the world is round."

The man shouted, "You lie. I am going to call the soldiers."

Tom took out the tape recorder. Then he said to the man, "Say something. Say anything at all."

The man said, "I will take you to the soldiers."

Tom played back what the man had said. "I will take you to the soldiers."

The man looked around the room. "Who said that?" He looked at the recorder. "A voice without a man!"

Tom explained the tape recorder. Then Eric said, "That big thing on the hill is our time machine. It brought us back here in time."

The man shook his head. Then he said, "You know things that I do not know. Why does the world look so flat if it is round?"

Tom pointed to a ship that was far out on the ocean. "Look at that ship. All you can see is the top part of it."

The man looked at the ship. "You are right," he said. "I cannot see the bottom part of the ship."

Tom said, "You cannot see the bottom part of the ship because the earth is round. If the earth were flat, you would be able to see the whole ship. The earth looks flat because it is very, very big. You see just a small part of it."

Then Eric said, "Tom, I just saw something go into our time machine."

"What was it?" Tom asked.

Eric replied, "It looked like a big white dog."

The man hit his fist on the table. "I would like to kill that dog. He is mean. And he always comes around my shack. He bit one of my men the other day."

Eric said, "What if that dog bumps against the handle? We'll never get home."

Eric and Tom ran from the shack. They ran up the hill to the time machine. The fat man was right behind them.

E Number your paper from 1 through 26.

Write the time for each event shown on the time line.
- 4 thousand years in the future
- 40 thousand years ago
- 3 thousand years ago

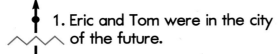

1. Eric and Tom were in the city of the future.

2. The year Thrig was from

3. Now

4. You were born.

5. Eric and Tom were in San Francisco.

6. The United States became a country.

7. Greece and Troy went to war.

8. Eric and Tom were in Egypt.

9. Eric and Tom saw a saber-toothed tiger.

10. Write the letters of 3 places that are in North America.
   - a. Japan
   - b. the United States
   - c. Mexico
   - d. Greece
   - e. Canada
   - f. Italy
11. Write the letters of 2 places that are in the United States.
   - a. Japan
   - b. Mexico
   - c. Italy
   - d. San Franciso
   - e. Ohio
   - f. Canada

Story Items

12. Let's say you saw a ship far out on the ocean. Would you be able to see the **whole ship** or just the **top part**?
13. Would you see **more** of the ship or **less** of the ship if the world was flat?

Skill Item

14. Compare object A and object B. Remember, first tell how they're the same. Then tell how they're different.

Object A   Object B

Review Items

15. Could all the people in the city of the future understand Eric and Tom?
16. Why could the old man understand them?
17. The people in the city of the future did not fix their machines. What fixed their machines?
18. The people of the future used such a simple language because ▆▆▆.
    - They were very smart.
    - They didn't think much.
    - They didn't like people.

19. In 1906, most of the streets in San Francisco were made of ▆▆▆.
    - tar
    - dirt
    - brick
20. Most of the houses were made of ▆▆▆.
21. The streetlights were ▆▆▆.
    - not as bright
    - brighter
22. Write the letters of the items that tell how people got from place to place.
    a. airplanes   c. wagons   e. trucks
    b. bikes   d. horses   f. buses

23. Which letter shows a horse from 40 thousand years ago?
24. Which letter shows a saber-toothed tiger?
25. Which letter shows a mammoth?

J   K   R

26. Where did Eric and Tom go after they left the cave people?

60

TEST 6

Number your paper from 1 through 36.

1. Write the letters of the 3 years that are in the future.

     a. 2099   c. 1990   e. 2020
     b. 1888   d. 1699   f. 2220

2. Write the letters of the 5 names that tell about time.
3. Write the letters of the 6 names that tell about distance or length.
4. Write the letters of the 2 names that tell about speed.

     a. days   h. feet
     b. minutes   i. hours
     c. centimeters   j. miles per hour
     d. inches   k. miles
     e. weeks   l. centimeters per day
     f. meters   m. yards
     g. degrees   n. years

5. Some buildings in Egypt are over ▮▮▮ years old.

     • 20 thousand   • 10 thousand   • 5 thousand

6. What is the name of the great river that runs through Egypt?
7. When kings and queens of Egypt died, they were buried inside a ▮▮▮.
8. When a person makes an object for the first time, the person ▮▮▮ the object.

9. Which letter shows where Turkey is?
10. Which letter shows where Greece is?
11. Which letter shows where Italy is?
12. Which letter shows where Spain is?
13. Which letter shows where Egypt is?

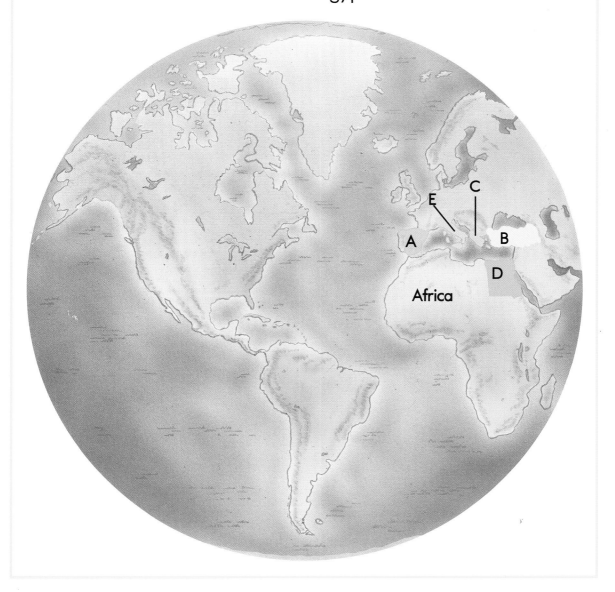

14. Write the letters of the 5 things that were invented after 1800.
    a. pyramids
    b. airplanes
    c. doors
    d. tape recorders
    e. buildings
    f. clothing
    g. rafts
    h. movies
    i. bicycles
    j. flashlights
    k. swords

15. Three thousand years ago, part of Greece went to war with ▓▓▓.
16. The war began because a queen from ▓▓▓ ran away with a man from ▓▓▓.
17. ▓▓▓ ships went to war with Troy.
    • 5 hundred   • 1 thousand   • 2 thousand
18. How long did the war last?

19. Write the letters that tell about a mammoth.
    a. long tusks
    b. long hair
    c. short tusks
    d. short hair
20. Write the letters that tell about a saber-toothed tiger.
    a. no ears
    b. long tail
    c. no teeth
    d. short tail
    e. long teeth

21. Write the letters of the 9 places that are in the United States.

        a. Italy
        b. Turkey
        c. Chicago
        d. China
        e. Alaska
        f. Denver
        g. Ohio
        h. Japan
        i. California
        j. Texas
        k. San Francisco
        l. Lake Michigan
        m. New York
        n. Egypt
        o. Spain
        p. Greece

22. Is the world round or flat?
23. Did Columbus think that the world was round or flat?

Write the time for each event shown on the time line.

24. Eric and Tom were in the city of the future.

25. The year Thrig was from

26. Now

27. Eric and Tom were in San Francisco.

28. The United States became a country.

29. Greece and Troy went to war.

30. Eric and Tom were in Egypt.

31. Eric and Tom saw a saber-toothed tiger.

Skill Items

For each item, write the underlined word from the sentences in the box.

> The <u>palace</u> <u>guards</u> spoke different <u>languages.</u>
> His <u>argument</u> <u>convinced</u> them to buy an <u>appliance.</u>

32. What underlining names the place where a king and queen live?
33. What underlining means he made somebody believe something?
34. What underlining names a machine that's used around the house?
35. What underlining refers to the words that people use to say things?
36. What underlining refers to what he said to convince people?

END OF TEST 6

61

A

1	2	3
1. George Washington	1. dirty	1. Viking
2. village	2. banging	2. whispered
3. probably	3. yelp	3. crouched
4. attack	4. sniffed	4. doesn't
5. Concord		
6. president		

B More About Time

Look at the time line. Touch dot C. That dot shows when Eric and Tom started their trip. What year was that?

Touch dot A. That dot shows when Eric and Tom were in the city of the future. When was that?

Touch dot B. That dot shows the year that Thrig was from. What year was that?

A ● Eric and Tom were in the city of the future.

B ● The year Thrig was from

C ● Eric and Tom found the time machine.

D ● Eric and Tom were in San Francisco.

E ● Columbus discovered America.

F ● Eric and Tom were in Greece.

G ● Eric and Tom were in Egypt.

H ● Eric and Tom saw cave people.

Touch dot D. That dot shows when Eric and Tom were in San Francisco. What year was that?

Touch dot E. That dot shows when Columbus discovered America. What year was that?

Touch dot F. That dot shows when Eric and Tom were in Greece. How long ago was that?

Touch dot G. That dot shows when Eric and Tom were in Egypt. How long ago was that?

Touch dot H. That dot shows when Eric and Tom saw the cave people. How long ago was that?

C The Dog and the Time Machine

Tom and Eric ran up the hill to the time machine. Tom looked inside. The big white dog was crouched down near the handle.

"Grrrrrr," the dog said, and Tom could see his teeth. The dog was very dirty and very skinny.

Eric looked inside and then whispered, "Tom, he's right next to the handle. If he bumps into that handle, the machine might disappear and we'll never get back home."

The fat man pushed past Tom and Eric. He was holding a big stick. "Let me at that dog," the man said. "I will give him a beating he will remember."

"No," Tom said and grabbed the man's arm. "Don't scare him."

The man looked at the inside of the time machine. He

looked at the dials. He watched the lights go on and off. Suddenly, he looked very frightened. "I have never seen such a thing as this machine," he said softly.

Tom hardly heard what the man said. Tom held out his hand. "Come here, boy," he said very softly.

"Grrrrrr," the dog said and showed his teeth again.

Tom turned to the man. "Do you have some food we can give the dog?" Tom asked.

"No, no," the man said. "I do not want to be around that dog or that machine." The man started to run back down the hill.

Eric said, "That dog doesn't like you, Tom. Let me talk to him."

Tom stepped out of the doorway. Eric went inside and moved toward the dog very slowly. The dog crouched lower and lower as Eric moved toward him. "Don't be afraid of me," Eric said.

The dog did not show his teeth. Slowly, Eric reached out and patted him on his head. The dog's tail wagged a little. Eric said, "You are a very nice dog."

Eric backed away ⭐ from the dog. "Come here," he said softly.

The dog stood up. His back was only about a centimeter from the handle. Tom could hardly watch. "Come here," Eric said again.

The dog took another step. Then he wagged his tail. His tail banged against the handle. "Oh, no," Tom said to himself.

But the dog's tail did not move the handle. The dog walked up to Eric. The dog jumped up on Eric and licked his face. "Tom, he likes me," Eric said.

Tom patted the dog on the head. Then Tom looked outside the time machine. The fat man was near his shack, talking to three soldiers. The fat man pointed toward the time machine.

Tom said, "We'd better get out of here. Take the dog outside."

"No," Eric said. "Those men might hurt him. We've got to take him with us."

The soldiers started running up the hill. Tom ran over to the seat and sat down. Swwwwwsssssh—the door closed.

A few moments later, a soldier was yelling and banging on the door. BOOM, BOOM.

Eric said, "Hurry up, Tom, before he breaks the door."

BOOM, BOOM, BOOM.

Tom grabbed the handle and pulled on it. It didn't move. The dog was crouched in front of the door. "Grrrrrr," the dog growled. Tom pulled on the handle. The handle moved.

The dials clicked and buzzed. The dog let out a little yelp. Then, as the force died down, the dog sniffed the air.

Eric said, "Tom, you pulled down on the handle. You should have pushed up."

Tom stood up and the door opened. The dog jumped back. The time machine was on another hill above water. And there was a ship down below them near the shore. The air outside was cool.

Tom pointed to the ship. "That is a Viking ship."

The Viking ship moved slowly along the shore of the ocean.

Number your paper from 1 through 23.

Tell about the dog that Tom and Eric found in Spain.
1. Write one word that tells about the size of the dog.
2. Write one word that tells about the color of the dog.
3. Write one word that tells how fat the dog was.

small	large	middle-sized	white
black	spotted	fat	skinny

Skill Items

Write the word from the box that means the same thing as the underlined part of each sentence.

stern	finally	crouched	faded
forever	buckle	bow	

4. The <u>front</u> of the ship was damaged.
5. The smoke <u>slowly disappeared</u> in the gentle wind.
6. <u>At last</u>, he finished the book.

Review Items

7. Write the letters of the 4 places that are in the United States.

        a. Turkey   e. Chicago   h. Denver
        b. China   f. Ohio   i. Alaska
        c. Mexico   g. Japan   j. Canada
        d. Italy

8. Which picture shows the smallest force?
9. Which picture shows the largest force?

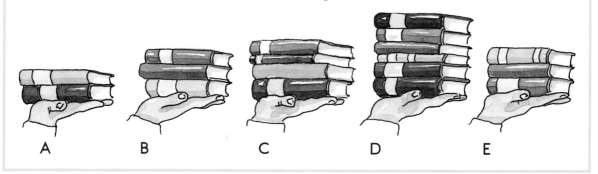

A   B   C   D   E

10. Write the letters of the 3 places that are in North America.

        a. Mexico   d. Canada   f. Spain
        b. Italy   e. Japan   g. United States
        c. China

11. Let's say you saw a ship far out on the ocean. Would you be able to see the **whole ship** or just the **top part?**
12. Would you see **more** of the ship or **less** of the ship if the world was flat?

13. What is it called when the sun comes up?
- sunset   • sunrise

14. What is it called when the sun goes down?
- sunset   • sunrise

15. Who discovered America?
16. When did he discover America?

17. Is the world **round** or **flat?**
18. Did Columbus think that the world was **round** or **flat?**

19. Which letter shows Italy?
20. Which letter shows Egypt?
21. Which letter shows the Nile River?

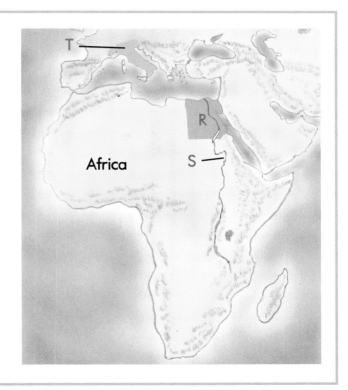

22. In what year did Eric fall into a crack in the earth?
23. A mile is a little more than ▮▮▮ feet.

62

A

1. helmet
2. voices
3. fighters
4. village
5. probably

B

Vikings

In today's story you will read about Vikings. Here are some facts about Vikings:
- Vikings were great fighters.
- Vikings sailed across the ocean to America before Columbus did.

- Vikings lived far north of Italy and Spain. The map shows where the Vikings lived.
- The Vikings lived where the winters are very long and cold.

C The Land of the Vikings

Tom and Eric were standing on the top of a hill looking at a Viking ship on the ocean below them. Tom figured that he and Eric were probably close to the year 1000. The Viking ship was moving slowly along the shore. Tom could hear the voices of the men on the ship as they sang. But he could not understand the words of the song.

As Tom watched the Viking ship, it turned and went out to sea. Eric asked, "Didn't the Vikings go to America before Columbus did?"

Tom said, "The Vikings sailed to America long before Columbus did."

Suddenly, the dog turned around and started to growl. Tom turned around. A very big man was behind them. The man was dressed in a robe made of animal skins. He wore a helmet with horns on either side.

"Grrrr," the dog growled.

The Viking looked at the dog and smiled. "Nur su urf," he said.

Tom said, "We can't understand your language."

The Viking pointed to the dog and smiled again. "Su urf," he said.

Eric said, "I think he's trying to tell us that he likes our dog."

The Viking touched Tom's shirt. "Su urf," he said. Then he pointed to the time machine. Again he said, "Su urf."

Eric said, "I think he likes everything, Tom."

The Viking waved his hand and then pointed. "Ul fas e mern," he said.

"He wants us to come with him," Eric said.

So Tom, Eric, and the dog followed the Viking into a grove of trees. They walked down a hill on the other side of the grove. At last they came to a little village. There were many huts and many dogs. The dogs started to bark.

The white dog growled at the other dogs.

People came from their huts and looked at Tom and Eric. The Viking who was walking with them told the people something and the people smiled.

A big gray dog came up to Eric and Tom's dog. Suddenly, the dogs started to fight and the Vikings started to cheer. Eric said, "Tom, stop them."

Tom moved toward the dogs, but a Viking grabbed his arm and shook his head. "In sing e tool," he said.

The dogs continued to fight. The gray dog was as big as

the white dog, and he looked stronger than the white dog. But the white dog was a little faster. Again and again the gray dog jumped at the white dog, but the white dog got out of the way. Both dogs became tired. The white dog had a cut on his neck. The gray dog's leg was hurt. Suddenly, the gray dog stopped fighting. He was about a yard from the white dog. He crouched down. The white dog started to move toward him, and the gray dog turned away.

All the people cheered. A woman ran over to the white dog. He growled at her, and everybody cheered again. Then she gave him a great big bone.

Tom said, "I think our dog just beat their best dog."

Three Vikings came over and patted Tom and Eric on the back. They led Tom and Eric to a large building. It was very dark inside the building. There were no windows, but there were many dogs and many tables. And it smelled bad.

The Vikings sat down at one of the tables. Tom and Eric sat next to them. Then some Viking women brought in great pieces of cooked meat. Each Viking took his knife and cut off a big piece. One of the Vikings cut pieces for Tom and Eric.

Eric said, "How are we supposed to eat? We don't have any forks."

Tom pointed to the Vikings. "Just eat the way they are eating." The Vikings were eating with their hands.

Suddenly, the dogs outside began to bark again. All the Vikings stopped eating. A boy ran into the building. "Left ingra," he yelled. The Vikings grabbed their knives and ran out of the building.

Number your paper from 1 through 24.

1. Which letter shows where the Land of the Vikings is?
2. Which letter shows where Italy is?
3. Which letter shows where Spain is?
4. Which letter shows where Greece is?
5. Which letter shows where Turkey is?
6. Which letter shows where Egypt is?
7. Which letter shows where San Francisco is?

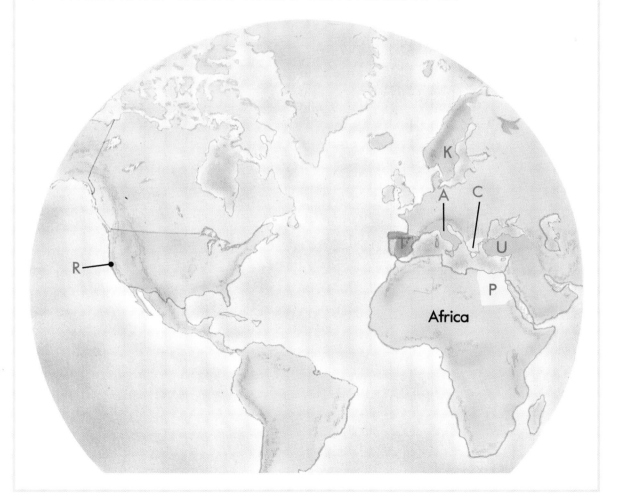

8. Who sailed across the ocean first, the Vikings or Columbus?
9. What were the winters like where the Vikings lived?

Skill Items

The army was soundly defeated near the village.

10. What word means **beaten**?
11. What word means **small town**?
12. What word means **completely** or **really**?

Write the word from the box that means the same thing as the underlined part of each sentence.

lowered	future	jungle	buried
survived	blade	tumbled	

13. The clothes <u>turned over and over</u> in the dryer.
14. Many strange plants live in the <u>warm, wet forest</u>.
15. Our dog <u>lived through</u> her illness.

Review Items

16. Where did the time machine take Eric and Tom after they left Egypt?
    • Greece   • San Francisco   • City of the Future
17. What was the teacher in the story wearing?

18. During the war between part of Greece and Troy, what kept the soldiers from getting inside Troy?
19. At last, the Greek army built a ████.
20. What was inside this object?
21. What did the men do at night?

22. How far back in time were Eric and Tom when they saw animals that no longer live on earth?
    - 40 thousand years in the future
    - 4 thousand years ago
    - 40 thousand years ago
23. Write the letters of 3 animals the boys saw 40 thousand years ago.

    a. saber-toothed tiger
    b. bear
    c. lion
    d. horse

    e. alligator
    f. pig
    g. cow
    h. mammoth
24. When did Columbus discover America?

63

A

1. wrestle
2. snowing
3. attacked
4. beard
5. flakes
6. outside

B **More About** Time

Look at the time line. Touch dot C. That dot shows when Eric and Tom started their trip. What year was that?

Touch dot A. That dot shows when Eric and Tom were in the city of the future. When was that?

Touch dot B. That dot shows the year that Thrig was from. What year was that?

Touch dot D. That dot shows when Eric and Tom were in San Francisco. What year was that?

Touch dot E. That dot shows when Columbus discovered America. What year was that?

Touch dot F. That dot shows when Eric and Tom were in the Land of the Vikings. What year was that?

Touch dot G. That dot shows when Eric and Tom were in Greece. How long ago was that?

Touch dot H. That dot shows when Eric and Tom were in Egypt. How long ago was that?

Touch dot I. That dot shows when Eric and Tom saw the cave people. How long ago was that?

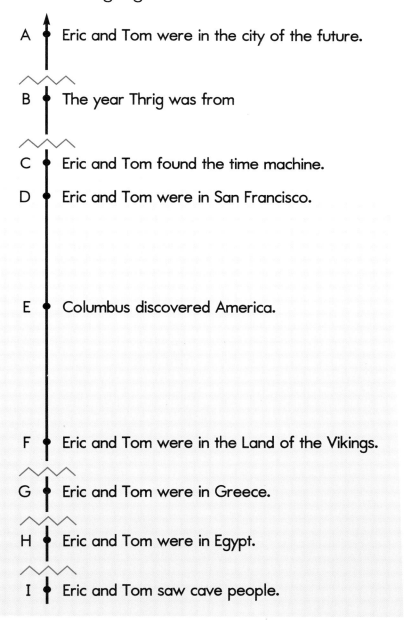

A • Eric and Tom were in the city of the future.

B • The year Thrig was from

C • Eric and Tom found the time machine.

D • Eric and Tom were in San Francisco.

E • Columbus discovered America.

F • Eric and Tom were in the Land of the Vikings.

G • Eric and Tom were in Greece.

H • Eric and Tom were in Egypt.

I • Eric and Tom saw cave people.

Trying to Get Home

Tom and Eric were inside the dark Viking building. Suddenly, the Vikings were fighting outside. The Vikings were using big, heavy swords and knives. Vikings from another village had attacked. These Vikings wore bands around their arms. Their leader was a huge man with a red beard.

Tom said, "I've got an idea." He started his tape recorder and ran outside. "Stop fighting! I am the god of sounds!" he yelled.

A Viking looked at him. "Un sur," he yelled.

Tom quickly played back the tape.

Some of the Vikings stopped fighting. They looked at Tom. Now more Vikings stopped fighting. Tom played the recording again and again. Soon all of the Vikings were looking at Tom.

One Viking raised his sword. His voice boomed out, "Esen trala."

Tom played back the Viking's voice: "Esen trala."

The Viking dropped his sword and stared at Tom. Then he turned to some of the other Vikings and said, "Su urf." The Vikings smiled. Then they started to laugh. They laughed and laughed. Some of them laughed so hard they almost fell over. The leader of the Vikings came over and grabbed Tom. He lifted Tom high into the air. All the Vikings held up their swords. "Sorta groob!" they shouted. "Sorta groob!"

The Vikings carried Eric and Tom into the dark building. All the Vikings sat down—the Vikings from both villages. There was shouting and yelling and dogs barking. Everybody ate and drank. For a long time, the Vikings sang and the dogs barked.

Then the Vikings went outside. Two Vikings started to wrestle. The other Vikings cheered, and the dogs barked. The two great Vikings rolled over and over on the ground.

Finally, the smaller Viking won. All the Vikings cheered. The Viking who lost stood up, smiled, and put one arm around the neck of the other Viking.

Later in the evening, Tom, Eric, and the dog walked back to the time machine. The Vikings followed. They sang.

Some of the Vikings looked inside the time machine. Then Tom motioned so that the Vikings would move away from the time machine. Tom sat down in the seat. The door closed.

Eric said, "Let's try to get to our year. I'm tired of going through time."

Tom pushed up on the handle. Dials started to click. Lights went on and off. Tom felt the force push against his ears. Then the force died down.

Tom stood up. The door opened. A blast of cold air came into the time machine. Outside it was snowing. The snow started to blow into the time machine.

Eric said, "Tom, let's get out of here. It's too cold out there."

Tom said, "How are we going to know where we are if we don't go outside and look around?"

Eric said, "But Tom, we'll freeze out there."

The time machine was on the top of a hill. The snow was coming down so hard that Tom could not see very far. He could see a grove of trees in the distance, but he couldn't see beyond.

Tom said, "I'll run to the grove and take a look. Maybe I can find somebody who can tell us the date. I'll be right back."

Tom ran from the time machine. He ran through the snow. It was deep and cold. His shoes filled up with snow. The cold wind cut through his shirt. Tom ran to the trees and looked into the distance. He didn't see anything.

But then Tom heard something. It sounded like a bell, very far away. So he ran through the trees toward the sound of the bell. He still couldn't see anything. And he was getting very cold. "I'd better get back to the time machine," he said to himself. He started to run back. The snow was coming down much harder now. Big fluffy flakes filled the air.

Tom ran back through the trees. Then he stopped and looked. He could not see the time machine. He called out, "Eric!" Then he listened. No answer. Tom was lost. The cold was cutting into his fingers and ears.

D Number your paper from 1 through 21.

Story Items

Here are some things the Vikings said:

    a. Su urf.   b. Ul fas e mern.   c. Left ingra.

1. Write the letter of the words that mean **I like that.**
2. Write the letter of the words that mean **Danger, danger.**
3. Write the letter of the words that mean **Come with me.**

4. Why did the Vikings like Tom and Eric's dog?

5. Compare object A and object B. Remember, first tell how they're the same. Then tell how they're different.

Object A   Object B

Review Items

6. Which arrow shows the way the air will leave the jet engine?
7. Which arrow shows the way the jet will move?

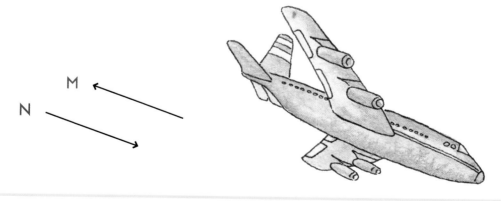

8. When a person makes an object for the first time, the person ▬ the object.

9. Who sailed across the ocean first, the Vikings or Columbus?

10. Write the letters of the 5 names that tell about time.
11. Write the letter of the one name that tells about temperature.
12. Write the letters of the 6 names that tell about distance or length.
13. Write the letters of the 2 names that tell about speed.

a. minutes
b. centimeters
c. years
d. inches
e. yards
f. miles
g. degrees
h. weeks
i. feet
j. miles per hour
k. hours
l. meters
m. feet per minute
n. days

14. Write the letters of the 9 places that are in the United States.
15. The United States is one country in North America. Write the letters of the 2 other countries that are in North America.

a. Japan
b. Turkey
c. Canada
d. Land of the Vikings
e. Alaska
f. Mexico
g. Lake Michigan
h. Greece
i. New York City
j. Texas
k. San Francisco
l. Ohio
m. Egypt
n. Denver
o. Spain
p. California
q. China
r. Italy
s. Chicago

16. Which letter shows where Italy is?
17. Which letter shows where Egypt is?
18. Which letter shows where Greece is?
19. Which letter shows where Turkey is?
20. Which letter shows where Spain is?
21. Which letter shows where the Land of the Vikings is?

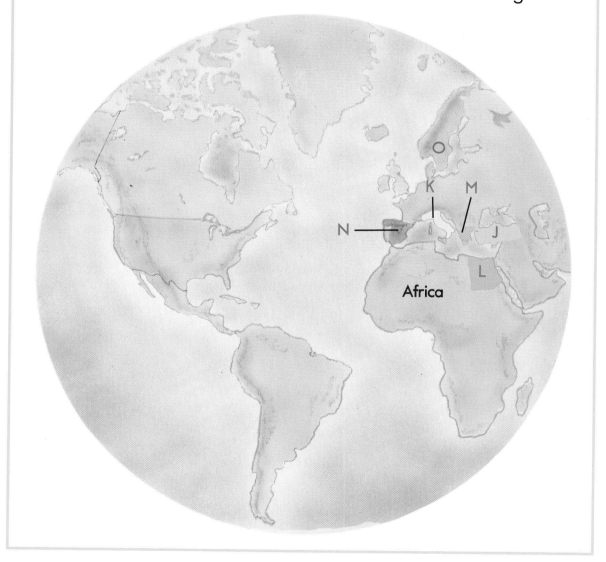

A

1
1. August
2. ashamed
3. kangaroo
4. double
5. Australia
6. microphone

2
1. valley
2. president
3. Robert
4. fireplace
5. Concord

3
1. wrapped
2. dying
3. studied
4. losing
5. marching
6. shooting

4
1. George Washington
2. spy
3. lad
4. church

B Facts About the United States

Here are facts about things that happened when the United States became a country:

- The United States had been part of another country called England.
- In 1776, the United States announced that it was a new country.

- England said the United States could not be a new country and went to war with the United States.
- The leader of the United States Army was George Washington.
- The United States won the war with England.
- George Washington became the first president of the United States.

C **Concord**

"I must keep moving," Tom said to himself. He was afraid. He started running through the deep snow. He could see his breath, but no footprints. The snow had almost stopped. The cold air cut through his shirt. He ran and he ran.

Suddenly, he stopped. In a valley below there was a little village. There was a horse and rider moving slowly down the street. A few people were standing in front of a church. The church bell was ringing—"gong, gong, gong." The village looked very peaceful.

Tom ran down the hill and into the village. Tom ran toward the people who were standing in front of the church. A man said, "You should be wearing a coat."

Tom said, "I'm . . . lost."

Another man said, "Come inside, lad."

The men took Tom into the church. Tom sat down near a fireplace. The heat felt good. Tom rubbed his hands together. Slowly, the cold feeling in his hands and feet started to go away.

Tom turned to one of the men and said, "What year is it?"

The man smiled. "Everyone knows what year this is. This is 1777."

Tom said to himself, "1777." Then he asked, "And where am I?"

"You are in the town of Concord."

Tom thought for a moment. The United States became a country in 1776. It was a year later now, and the United States was at war with England. The United States was losing the war.

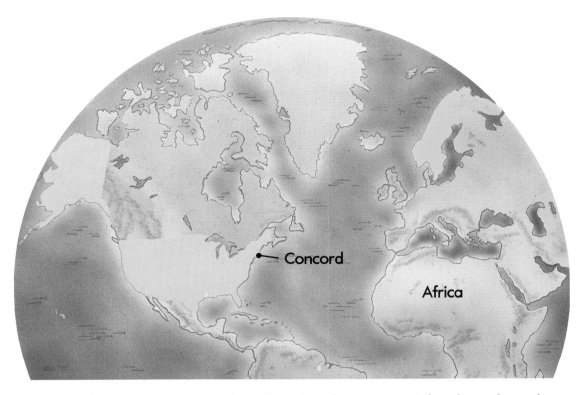

Concord

Africa

Just then, Tom heard a dog barking outside the church. The white dog was standing in the middle of the street. Tom ran up to the dog. "Where's Eric?" Tom asked.

The dog barked and ran down the street. Tom started to run after him. A man caught up to Tom and said, "Here." He handed Tom a big coat. It was made of fur. Tom put it on as he ran. The coat was very warm. The man who ran with Tom was tall and skinny. He took great big steps, and Tom had trouble keeping up with him.

"My name is Robert," the man said as they ran along.

They followed the dog up a hill and down the other side. Then they saw Eric. He was sitting in the snow, crying. He looked very cold. Robert took off his coat and wrapped it around Eric. Eric said, "I . . . I got lost." The dog licked his face. Eric patted the dog on the head.

Eric, Tom, and Robert started walking back to town. Eric studied Robert's clothes and said, "We are not in the right year, are we?"

Tom said to Eric, "I'll tell you about the year we're in. Right now, George Washington and his army are sick and hungry. Many of them are dying."

Robert said, "And Washington will not be able to make it through the winter. The English are going to win the war."

"No," Tom said. "The United States will win."

Robert laughed. "You talk like a fool. Some of Washington's men don't have shoes. They don't have food. How can they win a battle?"

Just as Tom was going to answer Robert's question, he noticed the town below them. He could see English soldiers marching into the town. They wore red coats. Robert said, "The English are looking for spies. If they find a spy, they shoot him."

Just then a shot sounded through the hills. One of the English soldiers dropped to the snow. Another shot sounded. The soldiers ran this way and that way.

Robert said, "Some of Washington's men are shooting at the English."

"Kazinnnnng." Something hit a tree next to Eric. Tom said, "Hey, the English are shooting at us."

"Zuuuuuuump." Another shot hit the snow near Tom. Tom yelled, "Let's get out of here."

Story Items

1. Which letter shows where San Francisco is?
2. Which letter shows where Egypt is?
3. Which letter shows where Greece is?
4. Which letter shows where the Land of the Vikings is?
5. Which letter shows where Concord is?
6. Which letter shows where Spain is?

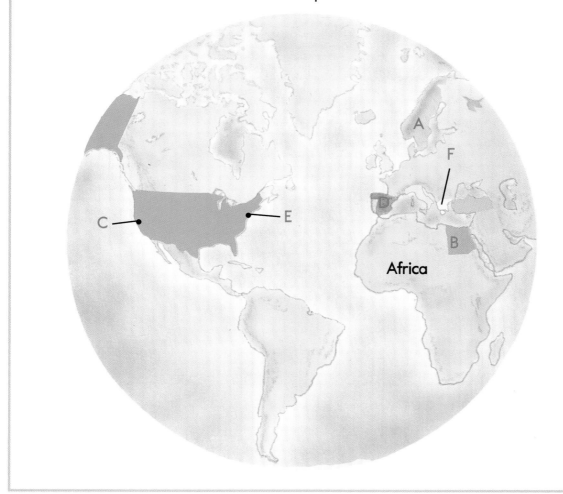

Here's a rule: **Birds are warm-blooded.**

7. Sam is not warm-blooded. So what else do you know about Sam?
8. A robin is a bird. So what else do you know about a robin?
9. A hawk is a bird. So what else do you know about a hawk?

Use the words in the box to write complete sentences.

| probably | defeated | attacked | appliance | argument |
| village | valley | convinced | soundly | studied |

10. His ▓▓ ▓▓ them to buy an ▓▓.
11. The army was ▓▓ ▓▓ near the ▓▓.

Review Items
12. How many legs does an insect have?
13. How many legs does a fly have?
14. How many legs does a bee have?
15. How many legs does a spider have?
16. How many parts does a fly's body have?
17. How many parts does a spider's body have?
18. In Egypt, Eric and Tom saw some huge stones on rafts. What were the stones for?

19. Why didn't the people in Egypt use trucks to haul things?

20. Write the letters that tell about a mammoth.
    - a. long hair
    - b. long tusks
    - c. short hair
    - d. short tusks

21. Write the letters that tell about an elephant of today.
    - a. long hair
    - b. long tusks
    - c. short hair
    - d. short tusks

22. Write the letters that tell about a saber-toothed tiger.
    - a. long teeth
    - b. short tail
    - c. no teeth
    - d. long tail
    - e. no ears
    - f. short teeth

23. Write the letters that tell about a tiger of today.
    - a. long teeth
    - b. short tail
    - c. no teeth
    - d. long tail
    - e. no ears
    - f. short teeth

24. When did Columbus discover America?
25. In what year did the United States become a country?

26. Let's say you saw a ship far out on the ocean. Would you be able to see the **whole ship** or just the **top part**?
27. Would you see **more** of the ship or **less** of the ship if the world was flat?

A

1
1. puzzled
2. creaked
3. cracked
4. August

2
1. described
2. dashboard
3. microphone
4. voice

B More About Time

Look at the time line. Touch dot C. That dot shows when Eric and Tom started their trip. What year was that?

Touch dot A. That dot shows when Eric and Tom were in the city of the future. When was that?

Touch dot B. That dot shows the year that Thrig was from. What year was that?

Touch dot D. That dot shows when Eric and Tom were in San Francisco. What year was that?

Touch dot E. That dot shows when Eric and Tom were in Concord. What year was that?

Touch dot F. That dot shows when the United States became a country. What year was that?

Touch dot G. That dot shows when Columbus discovered America. What year was that?

Touch dot H. That dot shows when Eric and Tom were in the Land of the Vikings. What year was that?

Touch dot I. That dot shows when Eric and Tom were in Greece. How long ago was that?

Touch dot J. That dot shows when Eric and Tom were in Egypt. How long ago was that?

Touch dot K. That dot shows when Eric and Tom saw the cave people. How long ago was that?

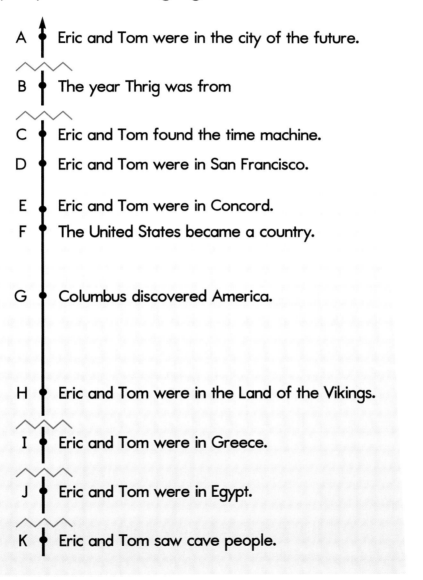

A — Eric and Tom were in the city of the future.

B — The year Thrig was from

C — Eric and Tom found the time machine.
D — Eric and Tom were in San Francisco.

E — Eric and Tom were in Concord.
F — The United States became a country.

G — Columbus discovered America.

H — Eric and Tom were in the Land of the Vikings.

I — Eric and Tom were in Greece.

J — Eric and Tom were in Egypt.

K — Eric and Tom saw cave people.

C   **Home**

Tom, Eric, and Robert were running from the English soldiers. After they ran about a mile, Tom stopped and said, "We don't know where we're going." He turned around. "But the dog knows." Tom bent down next to the dog. "Take us back to the time machine," Tom said.

Tom gave the dog a little push. The dog sniffed the air and then started to run. He stopped to sniff some animal tracks. He stopped to eat snow. But then he started to run in a straight line over the hills.

So Tom, Eric, and Robert followed the dog. Just when Tom began to think the dog didn't know where he was going, Robert said, "What is that thing ahead of us?"

Tom looked through the trees. "That's it. That's our time machine."

Tom, Eric, and Robert ran up to the time machine. Robert looked very puzzled. The time machine was filled with snow. There was so much snow inside that the seat was covered. Tom and Eric started to dig through the snow. They pushed most of it out of the time machine.

Then Tom turned to Robert. Tom said, "You'd better come with us. If the English soldiers find you, they'll kill you."

"No," Robert said. "I am going to fight the English. I will join Washington's army."

Eric took off Robert's coat and handed it to him. "You will need this," he said.

Tom took off his coat. He said, "And you can give this to one of the other soldiers."

Robert took the coats. He put one on and threw the other over his shoulder. "Good luck," he said.

Robert started running down the hill. Soon he had disappeared into the woods. Three soldiers in red coats were coming from the other direction.

Tom sat down in the seat. The door did not close. Tom said, "The seat must be frozen." He bounced up and down. The English soldiers were very close. The dog was standing in the doorway growling at them. One soldier came up to the doorway. "Come out of there," he yelled.

Eric pushed on the seat. Tom bounced up and down. Suddenly, the seat creaked and—swwwwsh—the door closed.

"Bong! Bong!"

"I hope the handle works," Tom said. He pulled on the handle, but it seemed to be frozen.

Tom banged on the dashboard. Suddenly, a door opened

and a microphone popped out. A voice said, "What year and month do you wish to go to?"

Eric and Tom looked at each other. "The month we want is August," Eric said. Then he told the year. The handle moved. Several dials lit up. Then the voice said, "What date in August?"

Eric said, "The 19th. It is a Saturday."

Again the end of the handle moved, and several more dials lit up. The voice said, "What time on August 19th?"

Tom said, "Make it about the time the sun goes down."

The voice said, "What place do you wish to go to on August 19th?"

Eric described the place. The voice said, "On August 19th, the sun sets at 8:32 P.M. in that place."

Eric asked Tom, "Who are we talking to?"

The voice said, "I am the computer that runs this time machine."

Suddenly, the force pushed against Tom. Then the force died down. Slowly, Tom stood up.

The time machine was on the mountain where Tom and Eric had found it. Tom could see the other kids walking home down the path below. As Eric and Tom started down the mountain, the time machine disappeared.

"Let's get out of here," Tom said. Tom yelled out to the other kids, "Hey wait for us!"

Tom, Eric, and the dog caught up to the other kids. Someone asked, "Hey, where did you get the dog?"

Tom smiled. "You wouldn't believe me if I told you."

Another kid asked, "What's the dog's name?"

Eric said, "Columbus."

"That's a silly name for a dog," one kid said.

Eric said, "It's not a silly name for this dog."

One of the girls said, "Let's go home. We've got a long way to go."

Tom laughed. "We don't have very far to go at all." Eric laughed too.

"Wow!" Tom said. "It sure feels good to be home." He patted Columbus on the head. Columbus wagged his tail. The lights were going on all over the town below. That town sure looked good.

The End

D Number your paper from 1 through 23.

Review Items

The speedometers are in two different cars.

A

Miles per hour

B

Miles per hour

1. How fast is car A going?
2. How fast is car B going?
3. Which car is going faster?

4. When the temperature goes up, the number of ▩
   gets bigger.
   - miles   • degrees   • hours   • miles per hour

5. When the United States announced that it was a
   country, England went to war with the United States.
   Who was the leader of the United States army during
   the war?
6. Which country won the war?
7. Which country was winning that war in 1777?

8. Who was the first president of the United States?
9. Who is the president of the United States today?

Write the letter that shows where each place is.

10. Italy
11. Egypt
12. Greece
13. Turkey
14. Spain
15. Land of the Vikings

16. Concord
17. San Francisco
18. Canada
19. United States
20. Mexico

21. Write the letter of the sun you see at noon.
22. Write the letter of the sun you see at sunset.
23. Write the letter of the sun you see early in the morning.

SPECIAL PROJECT

Make a time line that shows facts about your school and some of the people in it. Show the following events on your time line:

1. When the youngest student in your class was born.

2. When the oldest student in your class was born.

3. When you will enter high school.

4. When you will graduate from high school.

5. When your teacher or principal was born.

6. When your school was built.

You may want to show pictures of the people or things named on your time line. You may want to add other events that are important to your school or the students in your class.

A

1	2	3
1. finest	1. triple	1. kangaroo
2. breathed	2. Australia	2. joey
3. dusty	3. cloud	3. herd
4. ashamed	4. double	4. drunk
5. dancing	5. Toby	5. stomping
6. soundly		

B Facts About Australia

The story that you will read today begins in Australia. The map shows that the United States and Canada are on

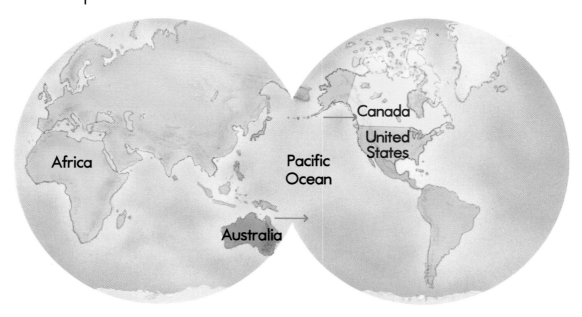

one side of the world. Australia is on the other side of the world.

Touch the United States.

Touch Canada.

Touch Australia.

Touch the United States again. Now go west from the United States.

What's the name of the ocean you go through when you go west from the United States?

The ocean that is west of the United States is the same ocean that is east of Australia.

Many animals that live in Australia do not live in any other place in the world. You can find some of these animals in zoos, but the only place you can find them living as wild animals is Australia.

Below are some animals that live in Australia.

platypus

kangaroo

koala

Toby the Kangaroo

This story starts in Australia, where Toby lived. Toby was a kangaroo. Like other kangaroos, he was part of a mob. A mob is a herd of kangaroos. There were over 50 kangaroos in Toby's mob.

Toby's mob was not the biggest mob in Australia and it was not the smallest, but it was like the other mobs in one way: It moved around from place to place. Every year, the mob would move in a great circle. The mob would stay in a place for a while, until the kangaroos had eaten the grass or drunk the water holes dry. Then the mob would hop, hop, hop to the next place where there was grass and water.

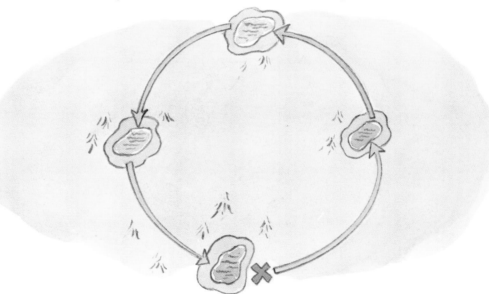

Those 50 kangaroos hop, hop, hopped on ground that was dry and dusty. Those kangaroos made a cloud of dust that you could see for many miles. When the ground was

very, very dry, the leader of the mob would be the first to hop along. Just behind the leader would be other kangaroos that were important in the mob. The kangaroos that were right behind the leader were more important than the kangaroos that came after them.

The leader did not have to breathe any dust. The important kangaroos that came right after the leader had to breathe a little bit of dust. The kangaroos that were not very important to the mob came last, right in the middle of the dust.

Toby was the last kangaroo in the whole mob. Toby breathed lots and lots of dust. When the leader said that the mob was going to move to another place, some of the kangaroos would cheer. Toby ★ did not cheer. He would say things like, "Oh, bad, double bad, and big bad."

If you looked at Toby, you might wonder why he was the very last kangaroo. He was a fine-looking kangaroo. He was strong. And he had the finest tail of any kangaroo in the mob. He was nearly as big as the biggest kangaroo in the mob, but Toby was just a boy kangaroo. The other kangaroos looked at Toby and said, "He is a fine-looking kangaroo. Too bad he's a joey."

A kangaroo does not like to be called a joey. A joey is a baby kangaroo. So when you call a big boy kangaroo a joey, you are calling him a big baby. Toby sure didn't like to be called a joey, but Toby was a big baby. He didn't work. He was always saying things like, "bad, double bad, big bad." The only two things he liked to do were eat and sleep. He could eat faster than anything you've ever seen eat. And he could sleep so soundly that he wouldn't wake up if the mob was singing and dancing and stomping all around him.

So Toby had to stay near the back of the mob as he hopped along and breathed dust. He kept mumbling, "Oh, double and triple bad." When the mob stopped for a rest, Toby had to listen to the other kangaroos call him a joey. Even Toby's mother was ashamed of him. She liked him, but she wished that he would grow up and stop being a joey. She did not know that very soon Toby would save the mob from kangaroo hunters.

Number your paper from 1 through 27.

1. Which letter shows where Australia is?
2. Which letter shows where the United States is?
3. Which letter shows where Canada is?
4. Which letter shows where the Pacific Ocean is?

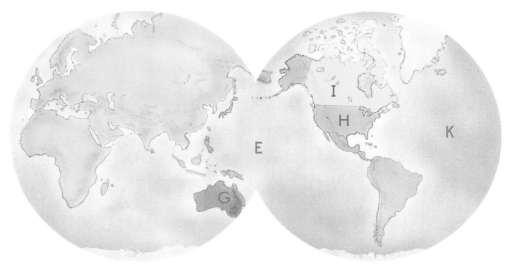

5. Which letter shows a kangaroo?
6. Which letter shows a platypus?
7. Which letter shows a koala?

Review Items

8. Jean is 16 miles high. Sue is 8 miles high. Who is colder?
9. Tell why.

10. Write 2 letters that show bulkheads.
11. Write 2 letters that show decks.
12. Which letter shows where the bow is?
13. Which letter shows where the stern is?

14. What is the temperature of the water in each jar?
15. Write the letter of each jar that is filled with ocean water.
16. Jar E is not filled with ocean water. How do you know?

32 degrees	32 degrees	32 degrees	32 degrees	32 degrees	32 degrees

A   B   C   D   E   F

17. Write the letter of the one name that tells about temperature.
18. Write the letters of the 6 names that tell about distance or length.
19. Write the letters of the 5 names that tell about time.
20. Write the letters of the 2 names that tell about speed.

a. meters per week
b. years
c. inches
d. minutes
e. feet
f. degrees
g. weeks
h. miles
i. meters
j. days
k. centimeters
l. miles per hour
m. hours
n. yards

21. Three thousand years ago, part of Greece went to war with ▓▓.
22. The war began because a queen from ▓▓ ran away with a man from ▓▓.
23. ▓▓ ships went to war with Troy.
   • 5 thousand   • 1 thousand   • 1 hundred
24. How long did the war last?

25. Which letter shows a mammoth?
26. Which letter shows a saber-toothed tiger?
27. Which letter shows a horse from 40 thousand years ago?

A   B   C

A

1	2
1. koala	1. lookout
2. ruin	2. pouch
3. India	3. warn
4. tough	4. honey
5. suit	5. forgotten
6. although	

B **Facts About** Kangaroos

Here are facts about kangaroos:

- There are many different kinds of kangaroos. Some kangaroos are as big as a man. Others are no bigger than a beagle.

- When a kangaroo is born, it is only three centimeters long.

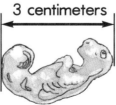

3 centimeters

PICTURE 1

- The baby kangaroo lives in its mother's pouch for half a year.

- Kangaroos have strong back legs and strong tails. In one jump, bigger kangaroos can jump over 10 feet. If a big kangaroo hit you with its tail, it would knock you down.

PICTURE 2

A Job for Toby

Toby was called a joey. Toby had to hop along through the dust at the back of the mob. And there were only two things that Toby really liked to do.

Just after the sun came up one day, the leader of the mob hopped over to where Toby was sleeping. The leader hit the ground with his tail. He hit it so hard that it made a thump you could hear two miles away. Although Toby could sleep through nearly anything, he woke up. The leader looked at him and said, "The time has come for you to stop being a joey. Today you are going to be a lookout." Then the leader asked, "Do you know what a lookout does?"

Toby said, "A lookout looks out for trouble." Toby was a little frightened. This was the first time the leader had spoken to him.

The leader said, "And what does a lookout do if there is trouble?"

Toby blinked. Then he said, "Smack your foot on the ground so that it makes a big noise."

"You are right," the leader said. Then the leader continued, "Go to the top of that hill and look out for a couple of hours. Then the mob will start moving."

Toby looked at the hill the leader pointed to. It was a very big hill. Toby was thinking about how hard it was going to be to climb to the top of that hill. But he didn't say anything, except, "Okay."

As Toby started up the hill, his mother hopped up to him. "Be careful, honey," she said. "Remember what happened to your ⭐ father."

"Oh, bad and big bad," Toby mumbled. He had almost forgotten about his father.

Years ago, when Toby was just a tiny kangaroo in his mother's pouch, Toby's father was a lookout. But he fell asleep and hunters caught him. Nobody in the mob ever saw his father again. But some of the kangaroos heard that he had been taken from Australia to another country, far across the Pacific Ocean. He was supposed to be in some kind of circus in that country.

Toby remembered his father. His father had the longest tail that any kangaroo ever had. And Toby's father had three large white spots on the top of his tail. Toby would never forget such a fine tail.

So Toby continued up the hill. He was getting so tired that he could hardly mumble, "Double, double bad." Finally, he reached the top, where he caught his breath. The sun was bright. The air was clear. There was no dust. When Toby sat down, he didn't mean to fall asleep, but he did. Toby really wanted to be a good lookout. He wanted to show the other kangaroos that he was not a big, lazy joey. But with the bright sun shining down, and that soft grass under him, he just rolled over, closed his eyes, and . . . zzzzzzzzz . . . zzzzzzzzz . . . . He was snoring away.

For a while, he was having a nice dream. Then he heard a voice in his dream. The voice said, "Don't wake that lookout. He'll warn the others." Suddenly, Toby realized that the voice was not part of a dream. He opened his eyes and looked around. Five hunters were sneaking past him on their way down the hill to the mob.

D Number your paper from 1 through 23.

Skill Items

1. Compare object A and object B. Remember, first tell how they're the same. Then tell how they're different.

Object A

Object B

Write the word from the box that means the same thing as the underlined part of each sentence.

continued	couple	thawed	boiling
announcement	argument	enormous	comparison

2. The snow <u>melted</u> when the sun came out.
3. The storm clouds were <u>very large</u>.
4. The teacher's <u>message</u> told about our homework.

Review Items

5. During the war between part of Greece and Troy, what kept the soldiers from getting inside Troy?
6. At last, the Greek army built a ▬.
7. What was inside this object?
8. What did the men do at night?

9. Write the letters of the 10 places that are in the United States.
   a. Australia
   b. New York City
   c. Chicago
   d. Alaska
   e. China
   f. Ohio
   g. Lake Michigan
   h. Japan
   i. Turkey
   j. Texas
   k. Land of the Vikings
   l. Italy
   m. Mexico
   n. Greece
   o. Spain
   p. Egypt
   q. San Francisco
   r. Concord
   s. California
   t. Canada
   u. Denver

10. If you go east from Australia, what ocean do you go through?
11. If you go west from the United States, what ocean do you go through?
12. What is a group of kangaroos called?
13. What is a baby kangaroo called?

14. Write the letters of the 5 lines that are one inch long.
15. Write the letters of the 5 lines that are one centimeter long.

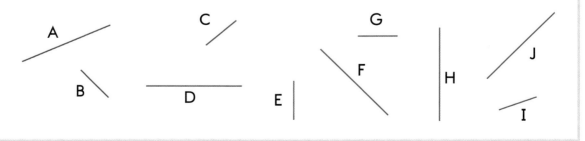

16. Which letter shows where Australia is?
17. Which letter shows where the United States is?
18. Which letter shows where Canada is?
19. Which letter shows where the Pacific Ocean is?

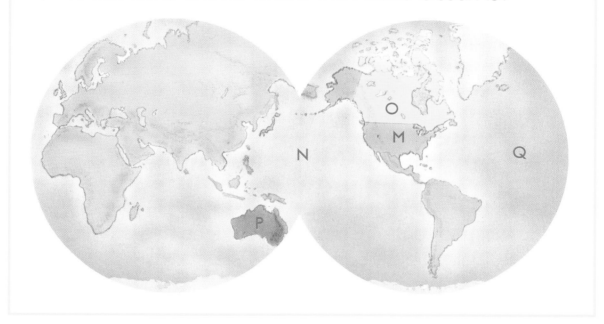

20. Is the world round or flat?
21. Did Columbus think that the world was round or flat?
22. About how many inches long is a meter?
23. How many inches long is a yard?

A

1	2	3	4
1. feather	1. <u>pea</u>cock	1. screeches	1. Mabel
2. spread	2. <u>color</u>ful	2. dark-colored	2. koalas
3. heading	3. <u>sail</u>ors	3. ruin	3. suit
	4. <u>sign</u>aled	4. tough	4. argued
	5. <u>tack</u>led		

B # Facts About Peacocks

You will read about a peacock in the next lesson. Here are facts about peacocks:

- A peacock is a large bird. A full-grown peacock is two meters long from its head to the end of its tail.
- The feathers of the male peacock are more colorful than the feathers of any other bird. When the male peacock shows off, it spreads out its tail feathers.
- The peacock is not a wild bird of Australia.
- The peacock has a very unpleasant voice. The peacock does not sing. It screeches.

The Kangaroo Hunters

Toby woke up and saw five kangaroo hunters. The leader was named Mabel. She was tough and nobody argued with her, not even the captain. The captain was the captain of a ship that was waiting about ten miles from Toby and the mob. The captain's sailor suit was too big for him and he kept pulling his pants up. The other three hunters were sailors from the ship.

Mabel ran a large circus in Canada. She was on a trip around the world to get animals—lots of them. She came to Australia to get kangaroos and koalas. She didn't plan to use all the animals that she caught. She planned to sell many of them to zoos or other circuses. She would keep the best animals.

When Mabel saw the mob down at the bottom of the hill, she knew that she was close to some very good animals. She sat down in the tall grass next to the captain. She whispered, "There's a big, dark kangaroo down there. We must get her."

"Yeah," the captain said in a loud voice.

"Be quiet," Mabel whispered. "If you wake up that lookout, you'll ruin everything."

"Oh, yeah," the captain said in a whisper and turned around to see if Toby was still sleeping. He seemed to be sleeping, but he wasn't. He was listening to everything Mabel and the captain were saying. He was pretending to be asleep because he didn't know what else to do. He didn't want to slam his foot against the ground because he was afraid that the hunters might shoot him. He didn't want to be shot.

"Come on," Mabel said as she put her binoculars away. "Let's sneak down this hill and get behind the mob. We should be able to catch ⭐ at least five kangaroos before they know we're around. Let's just make sure that we get that big, dark-colored one."

"Yeah, let's go," the captain said, and signaled his men to follow Mabel down the hill.

So there was Toby, pretending to be asleep as the hunters started to sneak down the hill. Below him was the mob. As Toby watched the hunters move down the hill, he said to himself, "Oh, great big bad. I can't let those hunters take kangaroos from my mob." Toby sat up. He lifted his foot into the air and he brought it down with a terrible smack. The sound echoed through the hills. For a moment, every kangaroo in the mob stood still, without moving and without breathing. Again, Toby signaled—smack.

This time, the kangaroos moved. And did they ever move fast. They all took off in the same direction at full speed. They made a cloud of dust that you could see all the way back at the captain's ship.

"Run, jump, get away from those hunters," Toby shouted as he smacked his foot against the ground again.

Mabel stood up, turned around, and looked at Toby. Then she shouted, "Well, there is <u>one</u> kangaroo that is not going to get away."

"Yeah, that's <u>right</u>," the captain hollered in a mean voice. The captain and Mabel were looking right at Toby.

"Oh, triple bad," Toby said to himself and started to hop down the other side of the hill. He went fast, but one of the sailors went faster than Toby went. By the time Toby reached the bottom of the hill, that sailor was right behind him. With a great leap, Toby tried to get away. With a greater leap, the sailor tackled Toby.

"We <u>got</u> him," Mabel yelled.

"Yeah," the captain said.

D Number your paper from 1 through 22.

Write the word from the box that means the same thing as the underlined part of each sentence.

important	although	confused	foul
motioning	constructing	opposite	normal

1. They finished <u>building</u> the house last week.
2. The garbage smelled <u>bad</u>.
3. She went to school, <u>but</u> she was sick.

Police officers checked the ship's cargo.
4. What words mean **cops?**
5. What word refers to the things that a ship carries?

Review Items
6. In what year did the United States become a country?
7. How many inches long is a yard?
8. About how many inches long is a meter?

9. Write the letters of 3 places that are in North America.
    a. Mexico   d. Greece   f. Japan
    b. Italy   e. United States g. Spain
    c. Canada

10. When did Columbus discover America?
11. Is the world **round** or **flat**?
12. Did Columbus think that the world was **round** or **flat**?

13. Which letter shows a kangaroo?
14. Which letter shows a platypus?
15. Which letter shows a koala?

16. What is the only country that has wild kangaroos?
17. How far can a kangaroo go in one jump?
18. A kangaroo is ▓▓▓ centimeters long when it is born.
19. Big kangaroos grow to be as big as a ▓▓▓.

20. Where does a baby kangaroo live right after it is born?
21. How long does it live there?

22. Toby's father had a tail that was different from any other kangaroo's tail. Name 2 ways that his father's tail was different.

69

A

1	2	3
1. preserve	1. strutted	1. India
2. officer	2. ramp	2. rainbow
3. break	3. clue	3. turkey
4. police	4. cargo	4. aren't
	5. minute	5. beauty

B Facts About Minutes

Today's story tells that Toby's eyes got used to the dark after a few minutes went by.

Here are facts about minutes:

- There are 60 seconds in a minute. If you count slowly to 60, one minute will go by.

- Some clocks have a hand that counts seconds. That hand moves fast. When that hand goes all the way around the clock, one minute goes by.

C Facts About Ships

In today's story, you will read about a ship. The picture shows the parts of a ship.

Ships carry things from place to place. Ships may carry grain or cars or machines. These things are called the **cargo.** A ship that carries grain has a cargo of grain.

The cargo is carried in a part of the ship called the **hold.** The hold is at the bottom of the ship.

D Toby on the Ship

Toby was in a cage, hanging from a long pole. Two sailors were carrying the pole—one at each end. Toby bounced up and down as the sailors walked. Next to them, the captain moved along, pulling up his pants every few steps. Mabel led the group. "Come on," she would holler from time to time. "Let's get moving."

"Yeah, get moving," the captain would say.

By the time Toby reached the ship, the sun was in the west. Toby hoped the sailors would let him out of the cage now. He said, "Oh, large and terrible bad," as he bounced along.

"Be <u>quiet</u>," Mabel yelled. The sailors carried Toby up the ramp and across the deck of the ship. The sailors put Toby's cage in front of a doorway that led down to the hold of the ship. Mabel yelled, "Put that kangaroo into the hold."

"Yeah," the captain said. "Into the hold."

The two sailors opened the door to the hold and tossed Toby down the stairs. It was so dark inside the hold that Toby couldn't see a thing at first. He looked to the left and looked to the right. He could smell other animals, but he couldn't see a thing.

Then, after a few minutes, his eyes got used to the dark and he could see the other animals. He could see three kangaroos and he could see something else. It was beautiful. Even in the dim light, its feathers shined like a rainbow. It was the biggest, most beautiful peacock you have ever seen.

The peacock puffed itself up. "Aren't I beautiful?" the peacock said. "Even in this terrible place, I am lovely, aren't I?"

"Oh, bad," Toby said to himself.

The peacock kept talking. "I'll bet that you felt bad when they threw you in here, but I know that you're happy now that you can see me. I was worth waiting for, wasn't I?"

"Oh, double bad," Toby said.

"Don't you just <u>love</u> my colors?" the peacock continued. "Of course, everybody knows that my tail feathers are the most beautiful things in the world, but look at some of my other feathers."

The peacock strutted out into the middle of the hold, where there was some sunlight that came through a crack. "If you want to see beauty, just take a look at these." The peacock turned around three times.

"Oh, triple bad," Toby said.

"Don't listen to that turkey," one of the other kangaroos said. The kangaroo continued, "That peacock will drive you nuts."

The peacock said, "I am <u>not</u> a turkey. I am the bird of India, the most beautiful thing in the world. I am not plain looking, like you animals from Australia."

Toby didn't want to talk about beautiful birds. He said, "When do we eat around here?"

The peacock said, "We get fed once a day. That won't happen until the sun goes all the way down, so you can still look at my feathers for a little while. That's better than eating anyhow."

"Oh, double bad," Toby said to himself. Then he turned to the other kangaroos and said, "Does anybody know where this ship is taking us?"

The peacock said, "I know and I'll tell you as soon as I show you something that you will remember forever." The bird puffed up and turned around very fast in the sunlight. Then he said, "Wasn't that something?"

Toby still didn't want to talk about beautiful birds. He said, "Where are we going?"

"I'll give you a clue," the peacock said. "The country we're going to is just north of the United States."

Toby said, "I don't know the name of that country."

The peacock said, "My, you animals from Australia don't know much. The country that is just north of the United States is Canada."

E Number your paper from 1 through 19.

Here's a rule: **Every plant is a living thing.**
1. A duck is not a plant. So what else do you know about a duck?
2. An oak tree is a plant. So what else do you know about an oak tree?
3. A boy is not a plant. So what else do you know about a boy?

Review Items

4. Let's say you saw a ship far out on the ocean. Would you be able to see the **whole ship** or just the **top part?**
5. Would you see **more** of the ship or **less** of the ship if the world was flat?

6. When the United States announced that it was a country, England went to war with the United States. Who was the leader of the United States army during the war?
7. Which country won the war?
8. Which country was winning that war in 1777?

9. Who was the first president of the United States?
10. Who is the president of the United States today?

11. A kangaroo that sits on a hill and warns the mob when trouble is coming is called a ▬▬.

12. What's the name of the large, beautiful bird of India with a colorful tail?
13. How many meters long is that bird from its head to the end of its tail?

14. What does a male peacock spread when it shows off?
15. Which is more beautiful, a peacock's feathers or a peacock's voice?
16. A kangaroo is ▬▬ centimeters long when it is born.
17. Big kangaroos grow to be as big as a ▬▬.

18. Where does a baby kangaroo live right after it is born?
19. How long does it live there?

Number your paper from 1 through 36.

1. Who sailed across the ocean first, the Vikings or Columbus?
2. How many seconds are in one minute?
3. Some clocks have a hand that counts seconds. When that hand goes all the way around the clock, how much time has passed?
4. The second hand on a clock went around 8 times. How much time passed?
5. What is the only country that has wild kangaroos?
6. How far can a kangaroo go in one jump?
7. A kangaroo is ▓▓▓ centimeters long when it is born.

8. Where does a baby kangaroo live right after it is born?
9. How long does it live there?
    - half a month
    - half a year
    - half a week

10. What's the name of the large, beautiful bird of India with a colorful tail?

11. Which letter shows where Greece is?
12. Which letter shows where Turkey is?
13. Which letter shows where Spain is?
14. Which letter shows where the Land of the Vikings is?
15. Which letter shows where Concord is?
16. Which letter shows where Canada is?
17. Which letter shows where Mexico is?

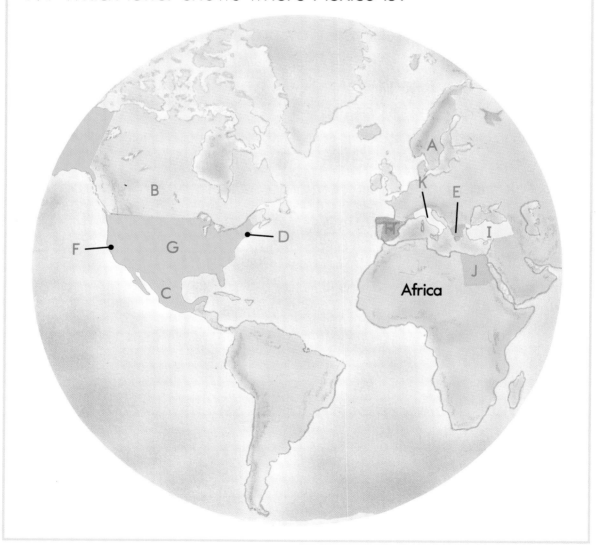

Write the time for each event shown on the time line.

18. Eric and Tom were in the city of the future.

19. Now
20. You were born.

21. Eric and Tom were in San Francisco.

22. Eric and Tom were in Concord.
23. The United States became a country.

24. Columbus discovered America.

25. Eric and Tom were in the Land of the Vikings.

26. Greece and Troy went to war.

27. Eric and Tom were in Egypt.

28. Eric and Tom saw a saber-toothed tiger.

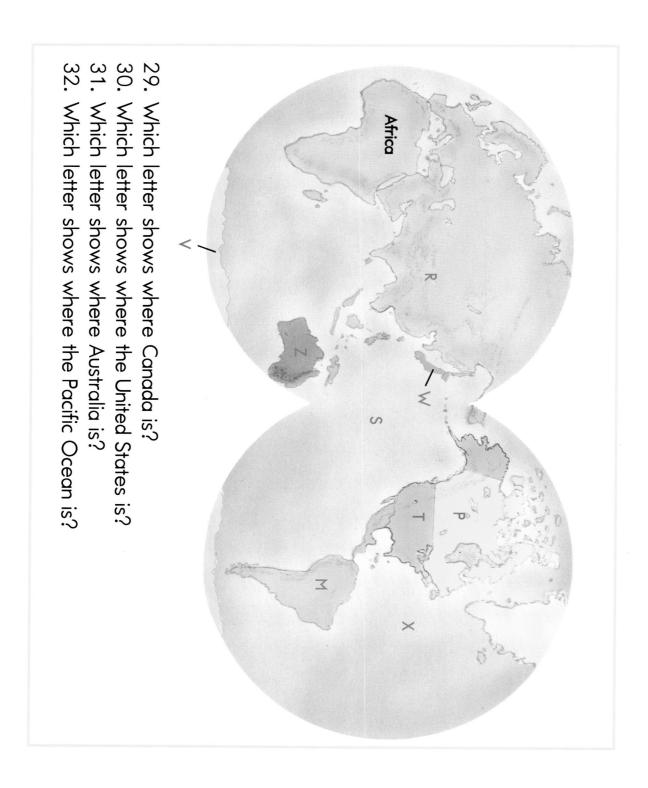

29. Which letter shows where Canada is?
30. Which letter shows where the United States is?
31. Which letter shows where Australia is?
32. Which letter shows where the Pacific Ocean is?

For each item, write the underlined word or words from the sentences in the box.

> The army was <u>soundly</u> <u>defeated</u> near the <u>village</u>.
> <u>Police officers</u> checked the ship's <u>cargo</u>.

33. What underlining means **beaten?**
34. What underlining refers to the things that a ship carries?
35. What underlining means a **small town?**
36. What underlining means **completely** or **really?**

END OF TEST 7

71

A

1	2	3	4
1. certain	1. <u>ca</u>mera	1. breaking	1. field
2. surprise	2. <u>foot</u>steps	2. liars	2. police
3. imagine	3. <u>blank</u>ets	3. crossed	3. law
4. recognize	4. <u>inter</u>esting	4. heading	4. untied
	5. <u>pre</u>serve	5. officers	
	6. <u>enter</u>tain	6. wiggling	

B

The End of the Trip

The ship was on its way to Canada. The peacock told the others that the trip would take ten days. "But don't worry," the peacock added, "I'll entertain you for the trip. You'll have a lovely time."

"Big and double big bad," Toby said to himself.

But before the trip was over, Toby had become friends with the peacock. The peacock's name was Pip. And Toby learned a lot from Pip. Pip knew the name of the ocean that the ship crossed. Toby had never heard of the Pacific Ocean before. Pip also knew a lot about the captain and Mabel.

On the day before the ship reached Canada, Pip told Toby, "Mabel and the captain are crooks. When you were in Australia you lived on a game preserve. It's against the law to hunt on a game preserve."

"Oh, that's double bad," Toby said.

Pip said, "Mabel and the captain are also liars. They pretended that they were going to take my picture with a camera. Mabel told me to stand in the middle of a field so that I would be in the bright sun."

Pip continued, "Then Mabel told me that the captain should stand behind me. That seemed like a good idea. The captain is so ugly that I would look twice as beautiful with him behind me. How did I know that he would drop a net over me?"

Toby mumbled to himself, "Not bad."

The next day was the day the ship was supposed to dock in Canada. There was a little hole in the side of the hold. The animals took turns looking out of this hole, trying to see the shore. Pip was looking through the hole just after noon. "My, my," he said suddenly. "I don't see the shore, but I do see something that is very interesting."

"What's that?" the other animals asked.

"I'll give you a clue. This thing goes through the water. It carries police officers. And it's probably looking for ships that are breaking the law."

Toby pushed the peacock out of the way and looked through the hole. He saw a police boat. And the boat was heading right toward their ship.

"We're saved," Toby shouted. "The police have caught Mabel and the captain."

"Not quite," the peacock said. "You'll discover that Mabel is very smart, even if she is a <u>crook</u>."

Two sailors ran into the hold.   The sailors slapped tape over the mouth of each animal. Then they quickly tied up the animals and covered them with large blankets. Then they dumped a pile of sacks on top of the animals.

Toby said to himself, "Very, very bad."

Toby could hear people talking near the doorway to the hold.

"What do you want, Officer?" Mabel said in a sweet voice.

"We're supposed to look at your cargo," the officer said.

"As you can see," Mabel said, "we're just carrying sacks of grain."

"Yeah," the captain said. "Sacks of grain."

Footsteps moved into the hold. Toby tried to make some sound by wiggling around.

The officer said, "Sounds as if you have rats in here. Better be careful or they'll get into your grain."

"Thank you, Officer," Mabel said. "We'll take care of the rats."

"Yeah," another voice said. "We'll take care of the rats."

Then the footsteps moved up the stairs. There was the sound of a door closing. A minute or two later, there was the sound of a motor that moved farther and farther from the ship Toby was on.

When one of the sailors untied the animals, Pip said, "What did I tell you? Mabel may be a crook, but she is very smart."

Things looked bad for Toby.

Number your paper from 1 through 21.

Skill Items

Write the word from the box that means the same thing as the underlined part of each sentence.

warned	scared	ruined	careful
largest	finest	screech	puzzled

1. The letter she got <u>confused</u> her.
2. The book was <u>destroyed</u> when it fell in the lake.
3. She didn't want the <u>most expensive</u> bike.

Use the words in the box to write complete sentences.

village	cargo	flight attendants	police officers
puzzled	defeated	dashboard	soundly double

4. The army was ▇▇ ▇▇ near the ▇▇.
5. ▇▇ checked the ship's ▇▇.

Review Items
6. If you go east from Australia, what ocean do you go through?
7. What does a male peacock spread when it shows off?
8. Which is more beautiful, a peacock's feathers or a peacock's voice?

9. What is a group of kangaroos called?
10. What is a baby kangaroo called?

11. Which letter shows the stern?
12. Which letter shows the hold?
13. Which letter shows a deck?
14. Which letter shows the bow?
15. Which letter shows a bulkhead?

16. What do we call the part of a ship where the cargo is carried?
17. Name the country that is just north of the United States.
18. How many seconds are in one minute?
19. Some clocks have a hand that counts seconds. When that hand goes all the way around the clock, how much time has passed?
20. The second hand on a clock went around 6 times. How much time passed?
21. A mile is a little more than ▒▒▒ feet.

72

A

1	**2**	**3**
1. illegal	1. roadside	1. graph
2. scolding	2. worthless	2. sped
3. awake	3. footsteps	3. pleasant
4. cannon	4. goodbye	4. arrives
5. thumping	5. gentleman	5. recognize
	6. peanuts	6. complain

B **Facts About** Canada

In the story you'll read today, Toby arrives in Canada. The map shows Canada.

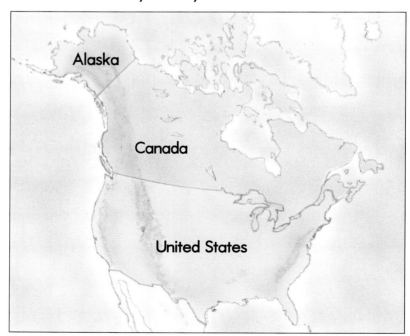

Here are facts about Canada:
- Canada is just north of the United States.
- Canada is colder than the United States.
- Canada is larger than the United States.
- Far more people live in the United States than live in Canada. The graph compares the number of people who live in the United States and Canada.

This bar shows how many people live in Canada.

This bar shows how many people live in the United States.

C The Ship Arrives in Canada

When the ship docked in Canada, it was night. Toby had been sleeping. He heard the sound of footsteps coming down the stairs to the hold. As Toby rubbed his eyes and tried to wake up, he realized that Pip was talking. Pip said, "I'll bet that they're going to try to sneak us into trucks and get us out of here before the police find out that there is illegal cargo on this ship."

Before Toby was completely awake, the three sailors had moved all the other animals from the hold. Toby was the last to go. He could hear Pip on the top deck, scolding the sailors. "Be careful with my feathers. Don't you recognize beauty when you see it?"

Three sailors started down the stairs for Toby. One of them tripped and fell into the other two. All three sailors fell into the hold. They began yelling at each other.

While the sailors yelled, Toby started to sneak up the stairs.

Just then, a loud voice from the top of the stairs said, "Throw a net over that kangaroo, you fools."

A moment later, a net fell over Toby. He tried to free himself, but he couldn't. The sailors hauled him up the stairs and dumped him onto a cart. "Take that kangaroo down the ramp," a voice yelled.

"Yeah, down the ramp," another voice said.

☾ A sailor started to push the cart down the ramp. Part

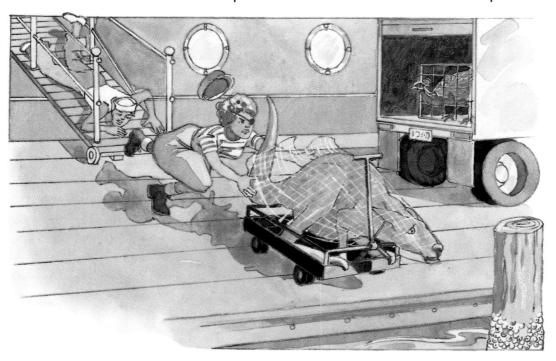

of the net got caught under the sailor's foot. The sailor tripped and fell forward. When he fell forward, he let go of the cart. The cart sped down the ramp. The cart continued to speed across the dock. It sped past a truck with the other animals in it. As Toby went by the truck, he could hear Pip saying, "Have a pleasant trip."

Toby's trip was not very pleasant. The cart came to the end of the dock, where there was a large post. The cart hit the post and sent Toby flying through the air. Toby flew right over the post. But the net caught on the top of the post and left Toby hanging above the water.

"Get that kangaroo," a voice hollered, and Toby could hear footsteps thumping down the dock. Then Toby felt the net being pulled up onto the dock. The sailors carried him to the truck with the other animals. Pip was saying, "Now be careful about my feathers. Don't push against me."

"Oh, triple bad," Toby said.

While it was still dark outside, the truck went to a circus. "This is where you get off," Mabel said to Toby. "You are going to be one of the stars of this tiny circus. You'll entertain people by being shot from a great cannon."

"Oh, many kinds of bad," Toby said.

The circus owner put a chain around Toby's neck and led him to a cage. Toby waved goodbye to Pip and the other animals. The circus owner told Toby, "Tomorrow, you will be a star. You will do tricks for people."

Toby didn't want to do tricks. He did not want to live in a cage and work for a circus. He wanted to be back home in Australia. As he sat there in that dark cage, he thought about the dust. The dust didn't seem very bad to him now. He missed the thumping sound of the mob. He missed the leader. Toby missed his mother and the other kangaroos. He missed the smell of grass and the sound of the wind.

As he sat there in his cage, he felt a large tear run down the side of his nose and fall off. "Oh, very bad," he said to himself and tried to go to sleep. Poor Toby even missed Pip.

D **Number your paper from 1 through 23.**

Skill Items

She paid the correct amount.
1. What word tells how much there is?
2. What word means **right?**

3. Compare object A and object B. Remember, first tell how they're the same. Then tell how they're different.

Object B

Object A

Review Items

Write the letter that shows where each place is.

4. Italy
5. Egypt
6. Greece
7. Turkey
8. Spain
9. Land of the Vikings
10. Concord
11. San Francisco
12. Canada
13. United States
14. Mexico

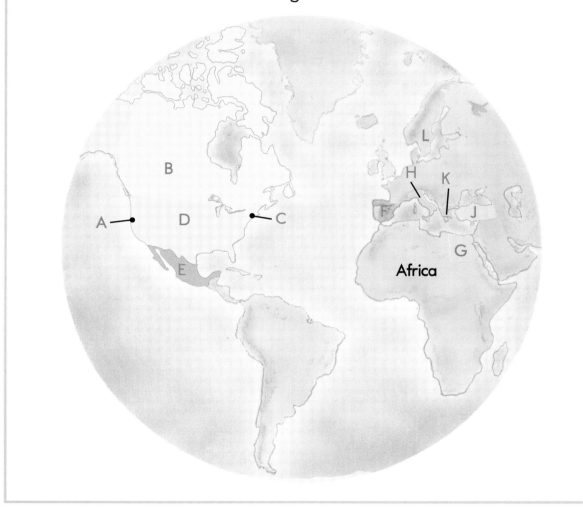

15. What is the only country that has wild kangaroos?
16. How far can a kangaroo go in one jump?
17. A kangaroo is ▇▇▇ centimeters long when it is born.
18. Big kangaroos grow to be as big as a ▇▇▇.

19. Where does a baby kangaroo live right after it is born?
20. How long does it live there?

21. How many seconds are in one minute?
22. Some clocks have a hand that counts seconds. When that hand goes all the way around the clock, how much time has passed?
23. The second hand on a clock went around 8 times. How much time passed?

A

1	2
1. <u>per</u>form	1. shabby
2. <u>pres</u>ents	2. rip-off
3. <u>rath</u>er	3. complaining
4. <u>um</u>brella	4. worse
5. <u>sur</u>prise	5. worst

B ## Facts About a Circus

In today's lesson, you're going to read about a circus that is not very good. People enjoy a good circus.

Here are some facts about a good circus:

- The circus is sometimes held in a large tent. The picture shows a huge circus tent.

- Two or three acts go on at the same time in a large circus. Some of the acts are on the ground. Other acts go on high in the air.

The favorite acts on the ground are trained animals and clowns. People like to see lions, tigers, and elephants do tricks.

The favorite acts in the air are people diving from one swing to another swing or people walking on wires.

A

B

Toby's New Job

The next morning, the circus owner came and took Toby from his cage. The owner said, "You are going to do tricks for the people who have come to see our circus. If you want to eat, you will do tricks. If you do <u>not</u> do tricks, you will become a <u>very</u> hungry animal."

Toby said, "Oh, bad and super bad."

The owner took Toby into a tent. In the middle of the tent was a ring.

"What a shabby circus," Toby said to himself.

This circus did not have many animals and people doing super things. Toby was the only animal in the tent. The owner was dressed up in a black suit with a rip in the back of the coat.

There was no huge crowd of people watching the act. There were about twenty people sitting in the stands. Three of them were sleeping. Two of them were little kids who were crying. The rest of them were complaining.

One girl said, "We want to see lions and tigers."

"Yeah," somebody else said. "We don't want to see a dumb kangaroo."

☾ The owner held up his hands. "This kangaroo can do tricks that will surprise you. This kangaroo is the smartest kangaroo in the world. People usually pay as much as a hundred dollars to see this kangaroo perform."

"Boo," the people yelled. "We want lions."

Then a girl yelled, "Make that kangaroo ride a bicycle."

"Make him ride it backward," a boy yelled.

The other people began to clap. "Yes, let's see him ride a bicycle backward."

"Wouldn't you rather see him being shot from a cannon?" the owner asked.

"No," the people agreed. "We want to see that kangaroo ride a bicycle backward."

The owner tried to argue with the crowd, but when people started to throw things at him, he said, "All right, he will ride a bicycle backward."

The owner got a dusty bicycle. He held up one hand and said to the crowd, "Ladies and gentlemen. Today the Kankan Circus presents Toby, the wonder kangaroo. Toby will amaze you by riding a bicycle backward. And he will do this amazing trick on a high wire ten meters above the floor."

Toby looked up at the wire ten meters above the floor. You know what Toby said.

The owner handed Toby the bicycle and said, "Take this bicycle up the ladder. ⭐ Then ride it backward on the high wire."

Toby shook his head, no.

The owner said, "<u>Do</u> it, you bad kangaroo. Get up there and ride that bicycle."

Toby shook his head, no.

The owner turned to the crowd. "Before Toby, the wonder kangaroo, rides the bicycle on the high wire, he will ride it backward on the floor." The owner turned to Toby. "Ride that bicycle on the floor."

Toby shook his head, no.

People were beginning to throw things at Toby and the owner. "This is a rip-off," they were hollering. "That kangaroo can't do anything."

The owner said, "One moment, ladies and gentlemen. Before Toby rides the bicycle backward on the floor, Toby will ride it forward on the floor."

The owner looked at Toby and said, "Do it." Toby shook his head, no.

People were now yelling, "I want my money back," and "Let's call a cop."

The owner held up his hands and said, "Before Toby rides the bicycle forward on the floor, Toby will walk with the bicycle on the floor."

Toby looked at the owner and shook his head no again.

"This is the worst show in the world," people were yelling. A woman was shaking her umbrella at the owner. Two boys were throwing papers at Toby. Toby was saying, "Oh, worse than bad."

D Number your paper from 1 through 25.

Skill Items

Write the word from the box that means the same thing as the underlined part of each sentence.

probably	sometimes	shabby	modern
suit	clean	helmet	pleasant

1. The clothes he wore were <u>not old-fashioned</u>.
2. We will <u>most likely</u> have chicken for dinner.
3. She wears a <u>hard hat</u> at work.

Use the words in the box to write complete sentences.

amount	finest	cargo	pouch
correct	pilots	tough	police officers

4. ▆▆▆ checked the ship's ▆▆▆.
5. She paid the ▆▆▆ ▆▆▆.

Review Items

6. Which direction would you go to get **from Canada** to the main part of the United States?
7. Which country is **smaller,** Canada or the United States?
8. Which country is **colder,** Canada or the United States?
9. Where do **more** people live, in Canada or in the United States?

Write the time for each event shown on the time line.

10. Eric and Tom were in the city of the future.

11. The year Thrig was from

12. Now

13. You were born.

14. Eric and Tom were in San Francisco.

15. Eric and Tom were in Concord.

16. The United States became a country.

17. Columbus discovered America.

18. Eric and Tom were in the Land of the Vikings.

19. Greece and Troy went to war.

20. Eric and Tom were in Egypt.

21. Eric and Tom saw a saber-toothed tiger.

22. Which letter shows Canada?
23. Which letter shows the United States?

24. When did Columbus discover America?
25. Who sailed across the ocean first, the Vikings or Columbus?

A

1
1. encyclopedia
2. hallelujah
3. truth
4. champions

2
1. refunded
2. worker
3. mountains
4. loudly

3
1. certain
2. roadside
3. stupid
4. imagine
5. boxer
6. amount

4
1. worthless
2. gloves
3. shoved
4. wear

B Facts About Boxing

The story in the next lesson will tell about kangaroos boxing. Here are facts about boxing:

- Two people box.
- The boxers wear large mittens called boxing gloves.
- The boxers box inside a place that is roped off. Although this place is not round, it is called a ring.
- The boxers hit each other with the gloves.

The fight ends if one boxer knocks out the other boxer. If one of the boxers does not knock out the other, the fight goes on for a certain amount of time.

C Toby Leaves the Circus

The circus owner refunded all the money the people had paid to see Toby. Then the owner led Toby back to his cage. The owner said, "You know how much you're going to eat, don't you?"

Toby knew how much he was going to eat. Toby sat there in his dark little cage, feeling very sad. He could hear the owner on the phone in the other room. The owner was saying, "You told me that the kangaroo could do all sorts of tricks. That stupid animal can't do anything. He has almost ruined my circus."

The owner stopped talking for a while. Then the owner said, "But I paid you a lot of money for that kangaroo. I want my thousand dollars back." Again the owner stopped talking. Then the owner said, "All right. It's a deal. But you and the captain are crooks."

Later that day, a truck came by. The owner led Toby into the truck. The captain and Mabel got out of the truck, and they talked to the owner for a few minutes. The owner looked very unhappy. Then the captain and Mabel got in the back of the truck with Toby. They were laughing. Mabel said, "We really tricked that circus owner."

The captain said, "Yeah, really tricked him."

Mabel said, "Imagine. We sold him that worthless kangaroo for one thousand dollars. Then we bought him back for one hundred dollars. Not bad."

"Yeah," the captain said. "Not bad."

Mabel said, "Now we'll sell that kangaroo to the Roadside Zoo for one thousand dollars and we'll make more money."

"Yeah," the captain said. "More money."

The truck left the city and drove for hours into the mountains. Then it stopped. Toby saw a sign, "Roadside Zoo." Toby saw other signs: "Amazing Animals," "Killer Snakes," "Apes," and "The Beautiful Bird of India." A worker was putting up a new sign. It said, "Boxing Kangaroos."

❀ One of the sailors led Toby into this zoo. The zoo smelled very bad. It wasn't the kind of zoo that has many animals. There were about ten animals. Each was in a small cage. One of them was talking very loudly. "How in the world can I entertain people if I don't even have enough room to spread out my lovely feathers?"

"Pip," Toby hollered.

But Toby didn't have a chance to talk with Pip. The sailor led Toby to the end cage, far from Pip. There was already another animal in this cage. It was a kangaroo—a ❀ big one. ★ The sailor shoved Toby into the cage.

In the distance, Mabel was saying, "And now you have two boxing kangaroos."

It was very crowded in that small cage. There were legs and tails all over the place. Toby could see two tails. One of them was very big. Along the top of that tail were three white spots. Toby looked at the tail and counted the spots. Then he looked at the kangaroo. There was only one kangaroo in the whole world that had a tail like that. "Daddy," Toby said. "Daddy."

For a moment, the large kangaroo stared at Toby. Then he said, "Are you my little Toby?"

"Yes, Daddy," Toby said. "It's me. They caught me and brought me here."

"Oh, son," Toby's father said, with a tear running down the side of his nose. "I am so glad to see you."

The two kangaroos hugged each other with their short little front legs. Then they talked. They talked about dust and blue skies and the mob and Australia. They talked about Toby's mother and the leader and the other kangaroos from the mob. Then Toby's father said, "Son, we've got to get out of this terrible place and go home."

Toby said, "Double good."

D **Number your paper from 1 through 20.**

Skill Items

The champions performed perfectly.

1. What word means **without any mistakes?**
2. What word means **put on a show?**
3. What word means they won the championship?

Review Items

4. Write the letters of the 5 names that tell about time.
5. Write the letter of the one name that tells about temperature.
6. Write the letters of the 6 names that tell about distance or length.
7. Write the letters of the 3 names that tell about speed.

a. degrees	f. hours	k. miles per year
b. minutes	g. weeks	l. yards
c. miles per hour	h. centimeters	m. years
d. meters	i. miles	n. inches per week
e. inches	j. days	o. feet

8. Write the letters of 3 places that are in North America.
   - a. Mexico
   - b. Italy
   - c. Greece
   - d. Canada
   - e. Japan
   - f. United States
   - g. Spain

9. Who was the first president of the United States?
10. Who is the president of the United States today?
11. In what year did the United States become a country?

12. Write the letters that tell about a mammoth.
13. Write the letters that tell about an elephant of today.
   - a. short tusks
   - b. long tusks
   - c. long hair
   - d. short hair

14. Write the letters that tell about a saber-toothed tiger.
15. Write the letters that tell about a tiger of today.
   - a. long teeth
   - b. long tail
   - c. short tail
   - d. no ears
   - e. short teeth
   - f. no teeth

16. When the United States announced that it was a country, England went to war with the United States. Who was the leader of the United States army during the war?
17. Which country won the war?
18. Which country was winning that war in 1777?

19. In what country are peacocks wild animals?
20. A mile is a little more than ▨▨ feet.

75

A

1	2	3	4
1. Mesozoic	1. jewels	1. <u>poster</u>	1. project
2. dinosaur	2. earned	2. <u>hallelujah</u>	2. bought
3. skeleton	3. handful	3. <u>powerful</u>	3. gentlemen
4. Triceratops	4. easily	4. <u>correct</u>	4. truth
5. Tyrannosaurus	5. prettier	5. <u>plenty</u>	5. champions
	6. peanuts		6. returned

B

The Big Fight

It was noon when three workers led Toby and his father from the cage to a small tent. There were about twenty people inside the tent waiting for the boxing kangaroos to put on their show.

One of the workers put boxing gloves on both kangaroos. Then the owner of the zoo stood between the two kangaroos and said, "Ladies and gentlemen— boxing kangaroos. You will see them box like champions. You will see them fight until one of them knocks the other out. They will use their gloves, but these powerful animals will also use their tails."

The owner of the zoo was right about some of the things he said but not all of them. The crowd did see the kangaroos use their gloves. The crowd also saw them use their tails. But the two kangaroos did not hit each other. They had a plan. Toby's father winked at Toby. That was the signal for the two kangaroos to swing their little front legs as hard as they could. They both hit the owner of the zoo. Then the kangaroos swung their tails as hard as they could. Both tails hit the owner at the same time and he went flying through the air.

Quickly Toby ran over to the people in the crowd. "Please, listen to me," he said, but they were not listening. They were clapping and cheering. "This is the best act we ever saw. What boxing kangaroos."

"Please listen," Toby said. "We were taken from Australia by crooks . . . ."

The people were still laughing and clapping. "What an act," they were shouting.

Suddenly, there was a terrible screech. The crowd became quiet. Then a very loud voice said, "The kangaroo is telling you the truth."

Toby said, "Good for Pip."

Pip was in his cage, but he had such a loud voice that the people could easily hear what he was saying. "I was taken from my home in India. For me, this was terrible. For you, of course, it is very nice because you get to look at me. But the people who brought us here are crooks. Somebody should call the police."

Somebody did call the police. By the time the police came to the zoo, four people were sitting on the owner so that he did not escape. The people had let out all the animals. One platypus kept shouting, "Hallelujah!" A small bear was eating a handful of peanuts. Toby and his father were standing next to Pip. And Pip was entertaining the people.

"Here's one that will amaze you," Pip said and turned around with his tail feathers shining. "Notice how the sunlight catches the feathers and makes them shine like jewels."

When the police started to take the owner away, the owner said, "You can't blame me for this. I bought these animals from Mabel."

"That's correct," Pip said. "Mabel is a crook."

The owner said, "I'll tell you where you can find Mabel and the captain." And he did.

• • •

Mabel is in jail. So are the captain and the three sailors.

Pip is still in Canada. When he thought about going back to India, he realized that there were many peacocks there, and some of them were even prettier than he was. So he decided that he would continue to entertain the people of Canada. He has a nice place in a real zoo. He has plenty of room to turn around, and to show off.

The platypus went back to Australia. All the way back he kept saying, "Hallelujah!" The police took the bears, the snakes, and the apes to their homes.

That took care of just about everybody except Toby and his father. They went back to Australia too, where they found their mob.

When the other kangaroos saw Toby and his father, they cheered. "Toby saved us from hunters," they shouted. "Hooray for Toby."

The leader said, "We are glad that two very important kangaroos have returned to our mob. Both these kangaroos have earned our thanks."

Now, when the mob moves from place to place, the leader hops first. Right behind him is a kangaroo with a very long tail that has three white spots on it. And right next to that kangaroo is a kangaroo that used to be called a joey. And right next to that kangaroo is Toby's mother.

And when the mob moves along, you may be able to hear one of the kangaroos saying, "Oh, good, good, good."

The End.

Number your paper from 1 through 21.

Skill Items

Here are three events that happened in the story.
Write **beginning, middle,** or **end** for each event.
1. Toby and his father were taken to a small tent.
2. The police arrived.
3. The other kangaroos cheered when they saw Toby and his father.

Review Items

4. Which letter shows a kangaroo?
5. Which letter shows a koala?
6. Which letter shows a platypus?

7. If you go east from Australia, what ocean do you go through?
8. If you go west from the United States, what ocean do you go through?
9. Some clocks have a hand that counts seconds. When that hand goes all the way around the clock, how much time has passed?
10. The second hand on a clock went around 3 times. How much time passed?
11. In what country are peacocks wild animals?
12. What is a group of kangaroos called?
13. What is a baby kangaroo called?
14. What's the name of the large, beautiful bird of India with a colorful tail?
15. How many meters long is that bird from its head to the end of its tail?

16. Which letter shows the stern?
17. Which letter shows the hold?
18. Which letter shows a deck?
19. Which letter shows the bow?
20. Which letter shows a bulkhead?

21. Write the letters of the 10 places that are in the United States.

a. Denver
b. Turkey
c. Chicago
d. China
e. Alaska
f. Italy
g. Lake Michigan
h. Japan
i. New York City
j. Texas
k. San Francisco
l. Ohio
m. California
n. Greece
o. Spain
p. Egypt
q. Land of the Vikings
r. Concord
s. Mexico
t. Canada
u. Australia

END OF LESSON 75 INDEPENDENT WORK

SPECIAL PROJECT

Make a large poster that shows some of the animals that live in Australia. You may find pictures of animals of Australia in an encyclopedia or in other books. Your teacher will help you find some good pictures.

Make copies of the pictures you find. Put the pictures on a large poster. At the top of the poster write the title of the poster. Write the name of each animal near the picture of that animal. Below each animal write some facts about that animal.

- ✦ Tell what it eats.
- ✦ Tell what color it is.
- ✦ Tell how big it is.

A

1	2	3
1. Atlantic Ocean	1. armor	1. earliest
2. Florida	2. dinosaur	2. Triceratops
3. Bermuda Triangle	3. layers	3. killers
4. Andros Island	4. Tyrannosaurus	4. Mesozoic
5. Africa		
6. engineer		

B

Piles

Here's a rule about piles: Things closer to the bottom of the pile went into the pile earlier.

Here's a pile:

Which thing is closest to the bottom of the pile?

So the shoe went into the pile first. The shoe went into the pile before the book went into the pile. The shoe went into the pile before the bone went into the pile.

Look at the cup and the bone. Which object is closer to the bottom of the pile? So which object went into the pile earlier?

Use the rule to figure out which object was the **last** one to go into the pile.

Use the rule to figure out which object went into the pile just after the shoe went into the pile.

C Dinosaurs

We use the rule about piles to figure out how things happened a long time ago.

Look at picture 1. It shows a large cliff. There are rows of stones and rocks and seashells. Each row is called a layer. The layers are piled up. That means the layers closer to the bottom of the pile came earlier.

Which layer went into the pile earlier, layer C or layer D?

☾ When we look at the layers of rock, we find skeletons of animals and shells of animals. In

PICTURE 1

layer B, we find strange fish and other animals that lived many millions of years ago. In layer D we find the skeletons of horses. Near the bottom of layer D, we find horses that are no bigger than dogs. Near the top of layer D, we find horses that are as big as the horses of today.

When we look at layer C, we find the skeletons of some very strange animals. These are dinosaurs. Some of the dinosaurs were much bigger than elephants. Other dinosaurs had great spikes on their tails. No dinosaurs are alive today. The only place we find their bones is in one of the layers under ground. That is layer C. We can't find dinosaur bones in layer B. We can't find them in layer D.

The layers of rock tell us a great deal about things that happened millions and millions of years ago. They tell us what it was like when the great dinosaurs walked on Earth. There were no horses, bears, elephants, or rabbits. There were no mice or cats. But there were many animals. Most of them were probably cold-blooded.

Some dinosaurs ate big animals. These dinosaurs were huge ✦ killers that could move fast. The ones that are found near the top of layer C stood almost 20 feet tall.

When we move above layer C, we find the beginning of animals that we know—horses, cats, bears, pigs. No layers show skeletons of humans. But if these skeletons were in the picture, they would be at the very top of the pile, in layer D.

Here's another fact about the layers: When we dig a hole in any part of the world, we find the same layers. If we dig a hole in Africa or in Canada, we find skeletons of elephants near the top of the pile. We find dinosaurs in the next layer down.

The layer that has dinosaur skeletons is called the Mesozoic. The layer that came after the Mesozoic is the top layer. The top layer has no skeletons of dinosaurs. This layer is still being laid down. We live at the top of the top layer.

PICTURE 2

Picture 3 shows two of the most important dinosaurs that lived in the Mesozoic.

The huge killer that lived late in the Mesozoic is named Tyrannosaurus. Tyrannosaurus was about 20 feet tall, twice as tall as an elephant. The dinosaur with the horns and the armor is named Triceratops. Tyrannosaurus did not have an easy time killing Triceratops.

PICTURE 3

Number your paper from 1 through 24.

Story Items

1. Write the letter of the layer that went into the pile **first.**
2. Write the letter of the layer that went into the pile **next.**
3. Write the letter of the layer that went into the pile **last.**
4. Which layer went into the pile **earlier**—B or C?
5. Which layer went into the pile **earlier**—A or C?
6. Write the letter of the layer where we would find the skeletons of humans.
7. Write the letter of the layer of dinosaurs.
8. Write the letter of the layer where we find the skeletons of horses.
9. What's the name of layer C?
10. Write the letter of the layer we live in.
11. Are there any dinosaur skeletons in layer D?

Use the words in the box to write complete sentences.

sailors	perfectly	amount	colorful
correct	champions	surprise	loudly

12. She paid the ▬▬ ▬▬ .
13. The ▬▬ performed ▬▬ .

Review Items

14. What part does the **F** show?
15. What part does the **L** show?
16. What part does the **H** show?
17. What part does the **K** show?

18. How many shells does a coconut have?
19. What is the juice inside a coconut called?
20. Name the country that is just north of the United States.

21. Write the letters of the 5 names that tell about time.
22. Write the letters of the 6 names that tell about distance or length.
23. Write the letter of the one name that tells about temperature.
24. Write the letters of the 2 names that tell about speed.

a. centimeter
b. minutes
c. years
d. inches
e. days
f. yards
g. weeks
h. degrees
i. meters per hour
j. miles
k. hours
l. miles per minute
m. feet
n. meters

A

1	2
1. <u>Flor</u>ida	1. Andros Island
2. <u>stormy</u>	2. Bermuda Triangle
3. <u>warn</u>ing	3. Atlantic Ocean
4. <u>Car</u>la	4. Edna Parker
5. <u>ex</u>plaining	

B

Edna Parker

Edna Parker was thirteen years old. She had been out on her father's ship before. But this was the first time that her father, Captain Parker, let Edna bring a friend along. This was going to be a great trip for Edna.

☽ On other trips, Edna had a problem. She became bored. There was never anything for her to do on the ship after it left the harbor. Sometimes she would sweep up or help with the meals, but most of the time she just sat around and looked over the side of the ship at the swirling water. With Carla along, Edna would have fun.

•   •   •

Captain Parker was explaining the trip to the two girls. He pointed to a map of Florida and the Atlantic Ocean as he spoke.

"We are starting from here," he said, pointing to the tip

of Florida. "We are going to follow this dotted line to an island called Andros Island." Captain Parker continued, "That means we will pass through a place where hundreds of ships have sunk or been lost. It's called the Bermuda Triangle." Captain Parker continued, "Many sailors say the Bermuda Triangle is the most dangerous part of the ocean."

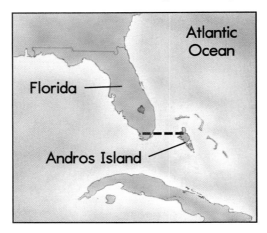

Carla's face seemed to drop.

"Hey," Captain Parker said, and smiled. "Nothing's going to happen in a big ship like this. We are very safe. And this is not the stormy season."

Carla asked, "Why is the Bermuda Triangle such a dangerous part of the ocean?"

"Bad seas," the ⭐ captain answered. Captain Parker said, "There are huge waves and storms that come up without any warning. And there are whirlpools."

Edna said, "You know what whirlpools are, don't you, Carla?"

"I think I know what they are," Carla replied.

Captain Parker said, "Let me explain. Did you ever watch

water that was going down the drain? Sometimes it spins around and around and it makes the shape of an ice cream cone."

"I've seen those," Carla replied. "They suck water right down the drain."

"Yes," Captain Parker said. "Those are tiny whirlpools. The kind of whirlpools that you find in the Bermuda Triangle are just like those, except they are big enough to suck a ship down."

"Wow," Carla said.

Edna was trying to imagine a huge whirlpool.

Captain Parker said, "Well, girls, Andros Island is only 120 miles from here, so we should arrive there in less than a day. We should have a smooth trip. The weather looks good. I am going to look over some maps now. You girls may play on deck, but stay away from the sides of the ship. And stay away from the lifeboats."

"All right, Dad," Edna said, and the girls rushed onto the deck.

main deck
map room
main deck
lifeboats

Number your paper from 1 through 24.

Skill Items

1. Compare object A and object B. Remember, first tell
how they're the same. Then tell how they're different.

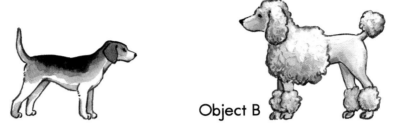

Object A   Object B

Review Items

2. Boxers wear large mittens when they box. What are
those mittens called?

3. Which object went into the
pile **earlier,** the knife or the
bone?
4. Which object went into the
pile **later,** the book or the
cup?
5. Which object went into the
pile **just after** the shoe?
6. Which object went into the
pile **just after** the pencil?

7. Which came **earlier** on Earth, dinosaurs or horses?
8. Which came **earlier** on Earth, strange sea animals or dinosaurs?
9. Write the letter of the layer we live in.
10. Write the letter of the layer the dinosaurs lived in.
11. What's the name of the layer the dinosaurs lived in?

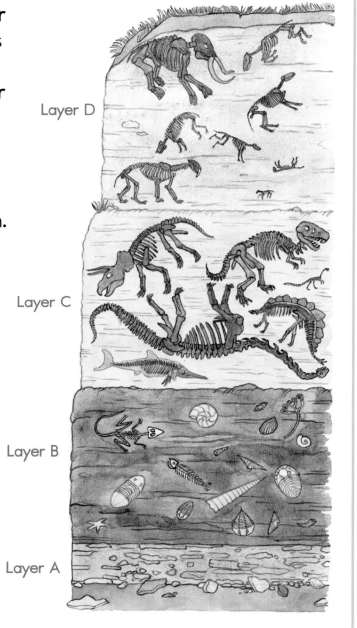

Layer D

Layer C

Layer B

Layer A

12. How many inches long is a yard?
13. About how many inches long is a meter?

Write the time for each event shown on the time line.

14. Eric and Tom were in the city of the future.

15. The year Thrig was from

16. Now

17. You were born.

18. Eric and Tom were in San Francisco.

19. The United States became a country.

20. Columbus discovered America.

21. Eric and Tom were in the Land of the Vikings.

22. Greece and Troy went to war.

23. Eric and Tom were in Egypt.

24. Eric and Tom saw a saber-toothed tiger.

A

1
1. seagulls
2. elevator
3. surface
4. pirates
5. instant
6. handkerchief

2
1. first mate
2. mast
3. engineer
4. silent
5. touch
6. pretend

3
1. exciting
2. powered
3. squawking
4. sliced

4
1. <u>hai</u>lstone
2. <u>spy</u>glass
3. <u>tip</u>toe

B **Facts About** Clouds

You're going to read about big storm clouds.
Here are facts about clouds:

- Clouds are made up of tiny drops of water.
- In clouds that are very high, the water drops are frozen. Here is how those clouds look.

- Some clouds may bring days of bad weather. These are low, flat clouds that stay in the sky for days.

- Some clouds are storm clouds. They are flat on the bottom, but they go up very high. Sometimes they are five miles high.

C Looking for Something to Do

Edna and Carla had dashed out of the map room. They had run to the stern of the ship, where they watched the seagulls that followed the ship. The girls watched the waves roll off the stern of the ship.

Then the girls ran to the galley. The cook was busy. They tried to talk to him, but the only thing he wanted to talk about was how much his new gold tooth hurt. After the girls spent about five minutes in the galley, they went to the engine room.

The engine room in a ship is the place where the ship's engine is. Some ships have engines that are as big as a school room. The engine of Captain Parker's ship was not that big. It was about the size of a small truck.

The engineer looked at the girls and said, "What do you think you're doing here?"

They told him that they were looking around. He replied, "If you want to stay here, I'll put you to work. So if you don't want to work, get out."

They left the engine room. They walked around the front deck. They thought about climbing the ladder that went up to the top of the mast. But that seemed too scary.

At last the girls sat down near a lifeboat. They sat and they sat and they sat. The girls tried to talk about different things. Edna studied the water. Then she realized that she was doing the same kinds of things that she used to do when she went alone on these trips. She was sitting in the sun watching the water.

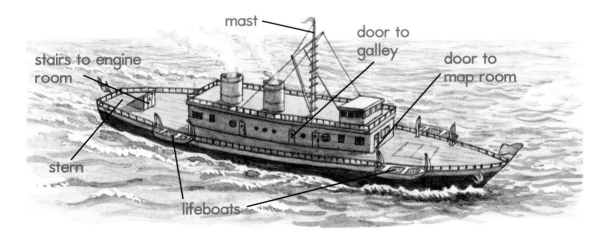

mast

door to galley

door to map room

stairs to engine room

stern

lifeboats

The sea was very calm, like a sheet of glass. The ship sliced through the water and left waves that moved out in a giant V as far as Edna could see.

There were beads of sweat on Carla's forehead. Carla said, "This Bermuda Triangle isn't as exciting as they say it is."

Edna nodded. "Yeah, this is boring."

For a moment, the girls were silent. Edna heard the squawking sound of the seagulls and the steady hum of the great engine that powered the ship. Then Carla said, "I wish we had our own boat. Then we could have some fun. I could be captain and you would be my first mate."

The girls looked at each other and smiled. Edna said, "Why don't we pretend that we have our own ship?"

Carla said, "I see a boat we can use for our game." She pointed to a lifeboat that was hanging at the side of the ship. It was ready to be lowered into the water in case of trouble.

Edna shook her head no. She said, "Remember what my dad told us? Stay away from the lifeboats."

"Oh, come on, Edna. We won't get in trouble if we are careful. We won't touch anything. We'll just sneak into the lifeboat and play for a while."

"No," Edna said slowly, looking at the lifeboat. Edna hadn't made up her mind to do it, but she looked around to see if any of the crew members could see them. She was just trying to figure out how hard it would be to sneak into the boat. No crew members were in sight.

"Come on," Carla said with a big smile. "Come on, Edna."

Number your paper from 1 through 19.

Story Items

After Edna and Carla left the map room, they went to different places on the ship.
1. Write the letter that shows where they went after they left the map room.
2. Write the letter that shows where they went next.
3. Write the letter that shows where they sat down in the sun.

Skill Items

Write the word from the box that means the same thing as the underlined part of each sentence.

they'd	spices	center	leaning
we'd	discovered	throne	hay

4. They put the table in the <u>middle</u> of the room.
5. The horses came running to get some <u>dried grass</u>.
6. <u>We would</u> rather play a game.

Review Items

7. Things closest to the bottom of the pile went into the pile ▇▇▇ .

8. Write the letter of the layer that went into the pile **first.**

9. Write the letter of the layer that went into the pile **last.**

10. Which layer went into the pile **earlier,** D or A?

11. Which layer went into the pile **earlier,** B or C?

12. Write the letter of the layer where we would find the skeletons of humans.

13. Write the letter of the layer where we find the skeletons of dinosaurs.

14. Write the name of layer C.

Layer D

Layer C

Layer B

Layer A

Use these names to answer the questions: **Tyrannosaurus, Triceratops.**

15. What is animal K?
16. What is animal L?

17. Captain Parker's ship passed through a place where hundreds of ships have sunk or been lost. Name that place.
18. Write the letters of the 3 things you find in the Bermuda Triangle.

    a. streams   d. whirlpools
    b. sudden storms   e. icebergs
    c. huge waves   f. mountains

19. What kind of animals lived in the Mesozoic?

A

1	2	3	4
1. shallow	1. <u>spy</u>glass	1. <u>e</u>levator	1. bailing
2. tearing	2. <u>sur</u>face	2. <u>for</u>ty	2. roughed
3. hind	3. <u>in</u>stant	3. <u>hand</u>kerchief	3. glassy
4. practice	4. <u>be</u>sides	4. <u>per</u>haps	4. tiptoed
			5. pirates
			6. sloshed

B

The Lifeboat

Carla and Edna were on the deck of Captain Parker's ship. Carla pretended to take out her spyglass and look around. "We're on an island," she said. "And there's our boat, pulled up on the beach." She pointed to the lifeboat. "I'm the captain and you're my first mate. So when I give an order, you carry it out."

Edna pulled off her shoes and socks and rolled up her pants to the knees. She tied a handkerchief around her head. She felt like a sailor now. "Yes sir, Captain, sir," she said as she stood up. The deck felt very hot on Edna's feet.

"Remember, we're on an island," Carla said. "We have to be very careful when we sneak into our boat. There are pirates on this island. Follow me."

Carla crouched down and tiptoed across the deck to the lifeboat. She climbed in the front. "The coast is clear," she said softly.

"Ouch, ouch, ouch," Edna whispered as she tiptoed across the deck. Edna jumped into the lifeboat. It rocked from side to side. It was held in the air by ropes that were attached to the bow and to the stern. Edna knew that you did something with the ropes to lower the boat into the water, but she wasn't sure how to do it. And she didn't want to find out.

For a moment, Edna had a bad feeling. They were doing something they shouldn't do. But then Edna explained things to herself. There wasn't anything else to do. None of the crew members would talk to them. And besides, they would be very careful.

Suddenly the boat dropped. Carla must have grabbed one of the ropes at the front of the boat or perhaps the rope just slipped. Edna didn't know. All she knew was that the boat was falling like a high-speed elevator. The ropes were making a howling sound as they ran through the wheels that had been holding the lifeboat. Edna wanted to yell something, but her voice wouldn't work.

☾ The bow of the boat hit the water before the stern. Edna held on to the side of the boat as hard as she could. But when the boat hit the water, Edna went flying forward, bumping into Carla. A huge wave broke over the front of the lifeboat and sloshed around in the bottom of the boat. The boat bounced in the waves that the large ship was making. Another wave broke over the side of the boat. For an instant, Edna was amazed at how loud the waves were. From the deck the ocean seemed almost silent. But now there were rushing sounds, splashing sounds, sloshing sounds. The waves from the stern of the big ship hit the lifeboat and almost turned it over.

Carla tried to stand up. She was waving her arms and yelling. Edna yelled, too. "Help!" "Stop!" "Here we are!" they yelled. The girls waved their arms. They continued to wave as the large ship became smaller, smaller, smaller.

Then the girls stopped waving and continued to watch the large ship. Now it was only a dot on the glassy water.

Suddenly, as the girls watched the dot, a very cool breeze hit them from behind. The air suddenly had a different smell. The wind roughed up the surface of the water.

Edna turned around and looked up. Behind the lifeboat was a great storm cloud. It rose up and up. "Oh no," Edna said. Then her mind started to work fast. "Let's start bailing water out of this boat. We're in for a storm."

When the girls started bailing there was about 5 inches of water in the bottom of the boat. The girls bailed and bailed. The waves got bigger and bigger. Now there was only about 3 inches of water in the boat, but the waves hitting the boat were very big and they were starting to splash over the side. The girls bailed and bailed and the waves splashed and splashed. Now there was about 4 inches of water in the boat.

The girls had to stop bailing when a terrible wind hit the boat. The waves were so large that Edna had to hang on to the side of the boat. She just kept hanging on and hoping that the storm would stop. But the waves were now over 20 feet high and the winds were moving forty miles per hour. The boat was going up and down the waves.

Number your paper from 1 through 29.

Write **beginning, middle,** or **end** for each sentence.
1. The girls had to stop bailing when a terrible wind hit the boat.
2. The ropes were making a howling sound as they ran through the wheels that had been holding the lifeboat.
3. Carla pretended to take out her spyglass and look around.

Review Items

4. What are clouds made of?
5. Write the letter of the storm clouds.
6. Write the letter of the clouds that may stay in the sky for days at a time.
7. Write the letter of the clouds that have frozen drops of water.

A   B   C

Write the letter that shows where each place is.

8. Turkey
9. Egypt
10. Greece
11. Italy
12. San Francisco
13. Land of the Vikings

14. Mexico
15. Spain
16. Canada
17. United States
18. Concord

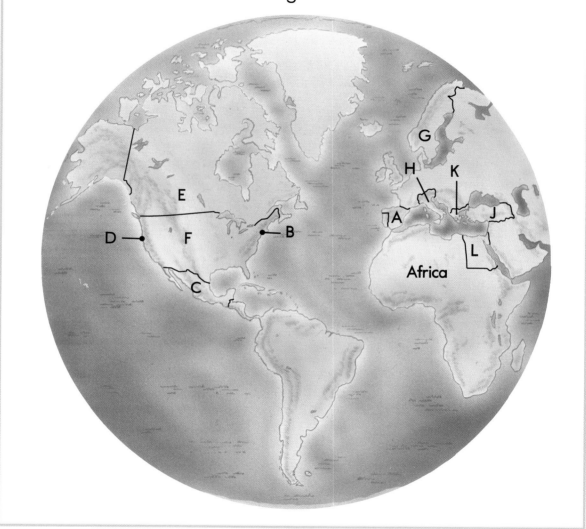

Write the time for each event shown on the time line.

19. Eric and Tom were in the city of the future.

20. The year Thrig was from

21. Now

22. You were born.

23. Eric and Tom were in San Francisco.

24. The United States became a country.

25. Columbus discovered America.

26. Eric and Tom were in the Land of the Vikings.

27. Greece and Troy went to war.

28. Eric and Tom were in Egypt.

29. Eric and Tom saw a saber-toothed tiger.

80 TEST 8

Number your paper from 1 through 33.

1. Which direction would you go to get from the main part of the United States to Canada?
2. Which country is **larger,** Canada or the United States?
3. Which country is **warmer,** Canada or the United States?
4. Where do **more** people live, in Canada or in the United States?

---

5. Which letter shows Canada?
6. Which letter shows the United States?

7. Things closest to the bottom of the pile went into the pile ▨ .

8. Write the letter of the layer that went into the pile **first.**
9. Write the letter of the layer that went into the pile **next.**
10. Write the letter of the layer that went into the pile **last.**
11. Which layer went into the pile **earlier,** B or A?
12. Write the letter of the layer where we find the skeletons of dinosaurs.
13. Write the letter of the layer where we would find the skeletons of horses.
14. Write the letter of the layer we live in.
15. What's the name of layer C?

16. Which object went into the pile first?
17. Which object went into the pile last?
18. Which object went into the pile earlier, the glass or the doll?
19. Which object went into the pile just after the book?

20. What are clouds made of?
21. Tell the letter of the storm clouds.
22. Tell the letter of the clouds that may stay in the sky for days at a time.
23. Tell the letter of the clouds that have frozen drops of water.

A   B   C

Use these names to answer the questions: **Tyrannosaurus, Triceratops.**

24. What is animal X?
25. What is animal Z?

For each item, write the underlined word from the sentences in the box.

> She paid the <u>correct</u> <u>amount</u>.
> The <u>champions</u> <u>performed</u> <u>perfectly</u>.

26. What underlining means **put on a show?**
27. What underlining tells how much there is?
28. What underlining in the second sentence means **without any mistakes?**
29. What underlining in the first sentence means **right?**
30. What underlining means they won the championship?

Here are three things you did as part of the test:
    a. You answered questions about clouds.
    b. You answered items about Canada and the United States.
    c. You answered questions about the meanings of words.

31. Write the letter of the thing you did near the beginning of the test.
32. Write the letter of the thing you did near the middle of the test.
33. Write the letter of the thing you did near the end of the test.

═══════ END OF TEST 8 ═══════

A

1	2
1. <u>thun</u>der	1. moaned
2. <u>shall</u>ow	2. funnel-shaped
3. <u>blind</u>ing	3. stumbled
4. <u>some</u>how	4. aloud
5. <u>light</u>ning	

B # How Hailstones Are Formed

You know that storm clouds are flat on the bottom and go up very high. Sometimes they are five miles high.

The arrows show how the winds inside storm clouds move. The winds move water drops to the top of the cloud. The drops freeze. When a drop freezes, it becomes a tiny hailstone. The tiny hailstone falls to near the bottom of the cloud. Here the tiny hailstone gets covered with more water. Then it goes up again and freezes again.

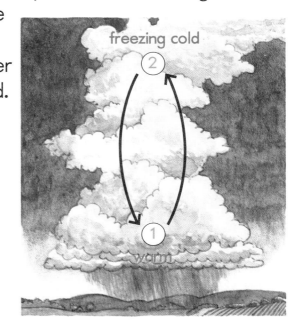

freezing cold
2
1
warm

Now the hailstone is a little bigger. It keeps going around and around in the cloud until it gets so heavy that it falls from the cloud. Sometimes it is as big as a baseball. Sometimes it is no bigger than a fingernail.

If you want to see how many times a hailstone has gone to the top of the cloud, break the stone in half. You'll see rings. Each ring shows one trip to the top of the cloud. Count the rings and you'll know how many times the hailstone went through the cloud.

| Hailstone A went through the cloud three times. | How many times did Hailstone B go through the cloud? |

Hailstone A

Hailstone B

C   A Giant Whirlpool

Now it was starting to rain. The small lifeboat was sliding up huge waves and then down the other side of the waves. Edna felt sick and dizzy.

When the boat reached the top of a wave, Carla shouted, "I see land." She pointed.

The lifeboat slid down the wave and Edna could not see anything but water. Then the boat moved up, up, to the top of another wave. Now Edna could see the thing that Carla had pointed to. But it wasn't land. It was a wave, much bigger than the other waves.

"Hang on," Edna shouted. "A giant wave is coming toward us."

For an instant, everything became bright as lightning shot through the sky. A boom of thunder followed. The huge wave was now very close to the boat. Edna looked up to the top of it. It was like a cliff of water with a white, foaming top.

Somehow, the boat moved up the huge wave—up, up, very fast. And now faster. The boat was moving so fast that Edna couldn't see what was happening. More lightning. Thunder. Edna had to close her eyes. She was dizzy. Dizzy.

The boat wasn't just moving up. It was moving around and around. The boat was moving so fast that Edna could hardly tell which direction was up and which direction was down. But she could see that the boat was on the top of a huge funnel-shaped cone of water. The boat was being sucked into a giant whirlpool.

Edna tried to say something, but her voice wouldn't work. She pointed down to the bottom of the whirlpool. It seemed to be hundreds of meters below the tiny boat.

 ☾ The next things happened very fast. They happened so fast that Edna was never sure exactly what happened or why. First, there were large hailstones—hundreds of them. For an instant, Edna noticed them floating in the boat, which was quickly filling up with water. So much hail came down that everything seemed to be white. The hail was hitting the girls, but Edna couldn't even feel it. Suddenly, there was a great flash and a great spray of water. The flash was blinding. Later, Edna thought a lot about that flash and the splash. Later she talked to Carla about it. The girls figured out that the lightning must have hit the water right in front of their boat. The lightning must have hit with so much power that it sent the boat flying through the air. After the flash was the giant splash. That must have been the splash that the boat made when it came down. The boat must have landed far from the whirlpool.

The hail continued to fall for a few minutes. Then it stopped, and a steady rain began to fall. For hours, the rain came down. The wind died down and the waves became smaller and smaller. Finally the rain stopped. Without any warning ✦ at all, it stopped. The sea was calm again, and Edna was sick. Edna didn't want to talk. She didn't want to move. She was dizzy. She was lying near the back of the boat. The boat was half-filled with water now. Edna moaned, "Ooooh." She wasn't sure she knew where she was anymore.

Carla was in the front of the boat, talking to herself. "I don't believe this," she said over and over. "I don't believe this. I want to go home."

Edna looked over the side of the boat. But she didn't see deep blue water that seemed to go down forever. She saw shallow water and sand. The boat was now in water that was only about a meter deep. Slowly, Edna looked around. "Land," she said aloud. She pointed to a row of palm trees and a beach that was about half a mile away. "Land," she said again. She was standing up and stepping over the side of the boat. "Land," she said and stumbled into the water. She fell down and got up and started to wade toward the trees. She wanted to be on land. She wanted to be on something that would not rock and bounce and make her dizzy. "Land," she said.

Skill Items

Write the word from the box that means the same thing as the underlined part of each sentence.

hooves	tame	modern	tusks
charging	English	ancient	

1. We visited the <u>very, very old</u> city.
2. My pet goat is <u>not wild</u>.
3. The hunters wanted the elephant's <u>large, curved teeth</u>.
4. We visited a very <u>new</u> city.

Use the words in the box to write complete sentences.

rescued	foul	eager	continued	normal
constructed	thaw	survived	occasional	

5. The ▆▆ ▆▆ smell was ▆▆.
6. She ▆▆ until she was ▆▆.

Review Items
7. What do we call the part of the ship where cargo is carried?

8. Which arrow shows the way the air will leave the jet engine?

9. Which arrow shows the way the jet will move?

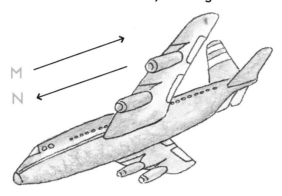

10. What part does C show?

11. What part does D show?

12. What part does A show?

13. What part does B show?

Use these names to answer the questions: **Tyrannosaurus, Triceratops.**

14. What is animal A?
15. What is animal B?

16. Which letter shows a kangaroo?
17. Which letter shows a koala?
18. Which letter shows a platypus?

19. In what country are peacocks wild animals?

20. Captain Parker's ship passed through a place where hundreds of ships have sunk or been lost. Name that place.

21. Write the letter of the layer that went into the pile first.
22. Write the letter of the layer that went into the pile last.
23. Write the letter of the layer that we live in.
24. What's the name of layer C?

Layer D

Layer C

Layer B

Layer A

82

A

1	2	3
1. upright	1. tangle	1. faint
2. overturned	2. gallons	2. hind
3. anyone	3. ignore	3. tearing
4. aloud	4. strangest	4. practice
	5. bending	5. crowded
		6. terrible

B

A Long Night

Carla called to Edna, "Help me get this boat on shore." The girls finally pulled the lifeboat onto the beach and turned it over. Many gallons of salt water spilled out and ran back to the ocean.

The sky was starting to clear. In the distance were heavy clouds, but the waves on the ocean were small. Behind Edna and Carla was a heavy jungle. A great tangle of trees and vines crowded down to the beach. From the jungle came the sounds of birds and other animals. The whole beach was covered with red sand. Edna had never seen sand like that before.

Edna walked a few feet from the overturned lifeboat and sat down on the soft, red sand beach. "I'm sick," she said.

"I'm sick, too," Carla said. She was lying down on the beach.

Edna rolled to one side. Carla was sleeping. Edna closed her eyes. The world seemed to be spinning around and around. The beach seemed to be rocking. "Oh," she said aloud. She kept her eyes closed and tried to ignore the terrible rocking and spinning.

• • •

"BRRRRAAAAHHHH!"

Edna sat up, her eyes wide. It was night. At first she didn't know where she was.

"BRRRAAAHHH!"

"What's making that noise?" Carla asked.

Edna turned toward Carla's voice. It was so dark that Edna could hardly see her.

🌙 Suddenly, as Edna looked in Carla's direction, she saw something moving out of the jungle. She heard it, too. It crashed through the vines and trees. There were breaking sounds and tearing sounds as small trees snapped and broke. Edna could see the faint outline of the trees being bent over and snapped down. Then she saw the faint outline of something else, something very large. An animal of some sort. "It can't be," Edna said aloud. The animal that she saw was too big. It was as big as some of the trees.

Edna didn't have much time to look at the animal because it stayed on the beach for only a few seconds. All Edna saw was a very faint outline. But she saw enough to know

that she was looking at an animal like nothing she had ever
seen before. It was big. It seemed to have a huge head.
And it seemed to walk upright, on its hind legs.

"BRRRRRRRAAAAAAHHHHH!" The animal seemed to
throw its head back when it roared. Then it suddenly
turned around and disappeared into the jungle. It left a
trail of great crashing and bending sounds.

"What was that?" Carla asked.

"I don't know, but I'm scared," Edna answered.

"Yeah," Carla said. "I think we ⭐ should go stay under the lifeboat."

"Good idea," Edna said.

So the girls crawled under the lifeboat and tried to sleep. But neither girl slept. One time, Edna was almost asleep when Carla moved her foot and made a noise. Edna sat up so suddenly that she hit her head on the inside of the lifeboat.

That was the longest night that Edna remembered. She kept waiting for the sky to become light. She wasn't sure which part would become light first, because she didn't know where east was. The first part to get light was over the jungle. Then it seemed that a year passed before it was light enough to see the ocean clearly. The sun was not up yet, but the birds were squawking and screaming in the jungle.

At last, Edna and Carla crawled out from under the lifeboat. The first thing they did was walk to where they had seen the outline of the huge animal. As soon as they got close to the spot, they saw the animal's huge footprints in the red sand.

When Edna looked at the footprints, she knew that there was an animal on this island that looked like no other living animal anyone had ever seen. It left footprints that were a yard long!

Number your paper from 1 through 17.

Skill Items

Write the word from the box that means the same thing as the underlined part of each sentence.

moan	excited	screech	box
certain	armor	pouch	surface

1. She put her keys in the <u>small bag</u>.
2. The <u>sharp sound</u> of the peacock startled me.
3. I am <u>sure</u> about the answer to the question.

Use the words in the box to write complete sentences.

returned	constructed	performed	warning
perfectly	easily	machine	lifeboat

4. The champions ▨▨ ▨▨.
5. They ▨▨ an enormous ▨▨.

Review Items
6. Which came earlier on Earth, dinosaurs or horses?
7. Which came earlier on Earth, strange sea animals or dinosaurs?

8. Write the letters of the things you find in the Bermuda Triangle.
   a. whirlpools   c. mountains   e. sudden storms
   b. streams   d. huge waves f. icebergs

9. Which object went into the pile **earlier,** the bone or the knife?

10. Which object went into the pile **later,** the book or the rock?

11. Which object went into the pile **just before** the pencil?

12. Write the letters of 3 places that are in North America.
    a. Mexico   d. Canada   f. United States
    b. Italy   e. Japan   g. Spain
    c. Greece

13. When did Columbus discover America?

14. What's the name of the large, beautiful bird of India with a colorful tail?

15. How many meters long is that bird from its head to the end of its tail?

16. What is a group of kangaroos called?

17. What is a baby kangaroo called?

A

1
1. breath
2. shriek
3. leathery
4. immediately

2
1. clearing
2. dents
3. driven
4. practiced
5. terrible
6. terribly

3
1. sense
2. pond
3. club
4. thick

4
1. groove
2. grove
3. steam
4. stream
5. tail
6. trail

B

Footprints

There was a row of footprints in the red sand. The footprints of the animal were a yard long. Each footprint had three toes. The size of the footprints told Edna something about the size of the animal. The footprints made very deep dents in the sand. These deep dents told Edna something about how much the animal weighed.

Between the footprints was a deep groove in the sand. Carla asked, "What could make that deep trail?"

Suddenly Edna shouted, "A tail. I'll bet a tail did that."

Edna continued, "That animal is walking on its hind legs. It's dragging a heavy tail behind it. The tail makes the groove in the sand."

For a while, the girls walked around the footprints and didn't say anything. Then they looked toward the jungle. The animal had left a huge path through the jungle. On either side of this path were thick vines and trees. But the path was almost clear. It looked as if somebody had driven a truck through the jungle and knocked down all the small trees and vines.

Edna said, "I don't think we should go into that jungle."

"Yeah, we shouldn't do it," Carla said. The girls were silent for a few moments. They just stood there and looked at the great path that led into the jungle. Then

Carla said, "But we could follow that path for a little way. We don't have to go too far."

"I don't want to go in there," Edna said. But she wasn't telling Carla the truth. Part of her was frightened and wanted to run away. But part of her wanted to see what made those huge footprints. Her mind made pictures of that animal. In one of the pictures, the animal was chasing Carla and Edna. Edna was running as fast as she could, but the animal was getting closer and closer and . . .

☾ "Come on," Carla said. "Let's go just a little way."

Now another part of Edna's mind was taking over. It wanted to see that animal. This part of Edna's mind was not terribly frightened. It made up pictures of Carla and Edna sneaking up on the animal. In these pictures, the animal did not see Edna and Carla. "This animal is not very smart," Edna said to herself. "If it was a smart animal, it would have found us last night. Maybe it does not have a good sense of smell. Maybe it has poor eyes."

"Okay, let's follow the path," Edna said to Carla. "But just a little way."

Carla picked up a short, heavy branch. She practiced swinging it like a club. Edna picked up a branch too. They were easy to find in the path made by the animal.

So the girls started down the path into the jungle. They walked very slowly and carefully. They jumped each time a screech or a roar came from the jungle. They tried not to step on small branches that would make a cracking sound. Slowly, they moved farther into the jungle. Soon,

Edna could not see the beach behind her. The trees over them blocked out the light.

"This is far enough," Edna said after she realized that the girls had gone over a hundred meters into the jungle.

"Shhh," Carla said, and pointed straight ahead. Edna could see a clearing. In the middle of it was a small pond. From the pond, steam rose into the air. The girls moved forward. Now Edna could see a small stream flowing into the pond. And she saw tall grass.

When the girls reached the edge of the clearing, Edna stopped. She noticed that the trees were very strange. She looked at a small tree on the edge of the clearing. "I saw a picture of a tree like this somewhere," she said. "But I can't remember where." She tried to remember. Suddenly, she did. And when she remembered, she wanted to run from the jungle as fast as she could. She had seen a picture of that tree in a book on dinosaurs. She had looked at the picture in the book many times. And she clearly remembered the tree. It was in a picture that showed Tyrannosaurus fighting with Triceratops.

Edna looked at the tree and remembered the huge footprints. "Oh no," she said aloud.

C Number your paper from 1 through 24.

Skill Items

The smell attracted flies immediately.
1. What word means **right now?**
2. What word means **really interested** the flies?

Review Items

3. Write the letters that tell about a mammoth.
4. Write the letters that tell about an elephant of today.

    a. short hair   c. long hair
    b. short tusks   d. long tusks

5. Write the letters that tell about a saber-toothed tiger.
6. Write the letters that tell about a tiger of today.

    a. short tail   c. long tail   e. long teeth
    b. no teeth   d. no ears   f. short teeth

7. Write the letters of the 2 names that tell about speed.
8. Write the letter of the one name that tells about temperature.
9. Write the letters of the 6 names that tell about distance or length.
10. Write the letters of the 5 names that tell about time.

    a. centimeters   f. miles   k. hours
    b. days   g. yards   l. miles per hour
    c. years   h. degrees   m. meters
    d. inches   i. inches per week   n. feet
    e. minutes   j. weeks

Use these names to answer the questions: **Tyrannosaurus, Triceratops.**
11. What is animal X?
12. What is animal Z?

13. A kangaroo is ▇▇▇ centimeters long when it is born.
14. Big kangaroos grow to be as big as a ▇▇▇.
15. A mile is around ▇▇▇ feet.

16. Write the letter of every line that is one inch long.
17. Write the letter of every line that is one centimeter long.

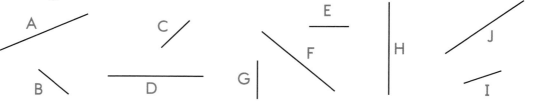

The speedometers are in two different cars.

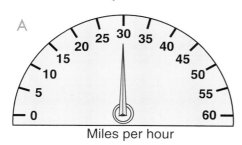

18. How fast is car A going?
19. How fast is car B going?
20. Which car is going faster?

21. Who was the first president of the United States?
22. Who is the president of the United States today?
23. In what year did the United States become a country?
24. Name the country that is just north of the United States.

A

1	2	3
1. <u>half</u>-folded	1. leathery	1. started
2. <u>ea</u>gle	2. breaths	2. stared
3. <u>for</u>got	3. instantly	3. sailed
4. <u>mon</u>ster	4. mouthful	4. slid
	5. immediately	5. spread

B

The Monster

Just as Edna was going to tell Carla about the tree in the book, a loud flapping sound came from the sky. A huge bird-like animal sailed down from above the jungle. It wasn't a bird because it didn't have feathers. It had large wings that looked like leather. The animal had large, sharp teeth. As the animal got close to the ground, Edna could see that it was very big—bigger than an eagle. The animal flapped its leathery wings loudly as it landed in the middle of the clearing. When it landed, the girls could see it more clearly.

Carla whispered, "What is that thing?"

Edna said, "It's an animal that lived a hundred million years ago."

Edna and Carla stared at the animal. It was on a rock with its wings half-folded and its mouth open.

"Let's get out of here," Edna said.

The girls began to sneak down the path toward the beach. Suddenly, the ground shook and there was a terrible crashing sound. The ground shook again. Edna couldn't tell where the sound was coming from. She ran from the path and hid behind a vine-covered tree. Then she realized that the crashing sound was moving closer and closer. It was coming from the beach and moving down the path toward the clearing. A small tree crashed to the ground right in front of Edna. Above her was the form of a monster. It was standing in the path that Edna and Carla had followed. Edna could smell the animal. It gave off a smell something like garbage. Edna instantly recognized the animal. Tyrannosaurus.

The monster moved so quickly that Edna could hardly believe it. Like lightning, it turned its head one way and then another. Its mouth was open and it seemed to be smiling with teeth as big as knives. The huge, bird-like animal in the clearing spread its wings and started to flap them. Immediately, Tyrannosaurus turned its head in the direction of the animal. An instant later, the monster was running toward the winged animal.

With each step, the ground shook. As Tyrannosaurus ran toward the clearing, its huge tail followed. It hit the tree that Edna was standing behind. The tree cracked. Edna went flying into the soft plants that covered the floor of the jungle. Before Edna could stand up, she heard noises from the clearing. There was a leathery flapping sound. Then there was a terrible crunching sound, like the sound of bones being crushed. There were three squawking sounds. Then there were more crunching sounds.

Edna got up and started to run. She ran down the path toward the beach. She made her legs move as fast as they could. And she kept telling them to move faster. She told herself, "Get out of here. Get out of here." She tripped and almost fell. "Don't fall," she told herself. "Run," she told herself. "Run and don't stop."

She wasn't thinking about the noise she made as she ran. She wasn't thinking that Tyrannosaurus might hear her. She wasn't thinking about anything but running. "Run," she told herself. "Don't slow down."

She noticed that there was a large snake on the path right in front of her. It was yellow and black, and it was at least three meters long. But she didn't even slow down. With a great leap she jumped over the snake and kept on running. When the girls had gone into the jungle, the path had seemed long. Now it seemed longer. It seemed as if it would never end. "Run," she said out loud between her breaths. "Run. Run."

Edna ran until she could see the beach ahead of her. Then her mind slowly began to work again. She stopped and turned around. There was nothing on the path behind her. Good. Good. Tyrannosaurus was making so much noise eating that flying animal that it couldn't hear Edna. Besides, Tyrannosaurus already had a meal. What would it want with a tiny animal like Edna? Edna wouldn't be much more than a mouthful for the monster. Edna was thinking now. She walked out onto the red sand of the beach.

She was out of breath. Now she began to realize how frightened she had been. She had been so frightened that she forgot about everything. She forgot about being careful. Suddenly, Edna turned all the way around. She had forgotten about Carla. Where was Carla?

Edna looked in all directions, but she couldn't see Carla.

C Number your paper from 1 through 23.

Here are three events that happened in the story:
- Write **beginning, middle,** or **end** for each event.
  1. Edna went flying into the soft plants that covered the floor of the jungle.
  2. A huge bird-like animal sailed down from above the jungle.
  3. She had been so frightened that she forgot about everything.

Review Items

4. Write the letters of the 10 places that are in the United States.

a. Denver	l. Ohio
b. Turkey	m. California
c. Chicago	n. Greece
d. China	o. Spain
e. Alaska	p. Egypt
f. Italy	q. Land of the Vikings
g. Lake Michigan	r. Concord
h. Japan	s. Mexico
i. Australia	t. Canada
j. Texas	u. New York City
k. San Francisco	

5. When did Columbus discover America?

6. Write the letters of the 3 places that are in North America.
    a. Canada   d. Mexico   f. Japan
    b. Greece   e. United States   g. Spain
    c. Italy

7. Write the letter of the footprint made by the lightest animal.
8. Write the letter of the footprint made by the heaviest animal.

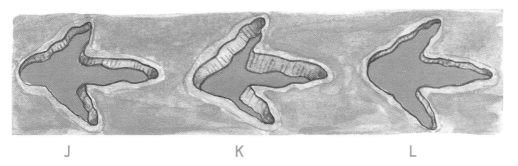

J   K   L

9. Tom is 8 miles high. Joe is 3 miles high. Who is colder?
10. Tell why.

11. How many legs does an insect have?
12. How many legs does a fly have?
13. How many legs does a bee have?
14. How many legs does a spider have?
15. How many parts does a spider's body have?
16. How many parts does a fly's body have?

The picture shows marks left by an animal.

17. Which arrow shows the direction the animal is moving?
18. Write the letter of the part that shows a footprint.
19. Write the letter of the part that shows the mark left by the animal's tail.

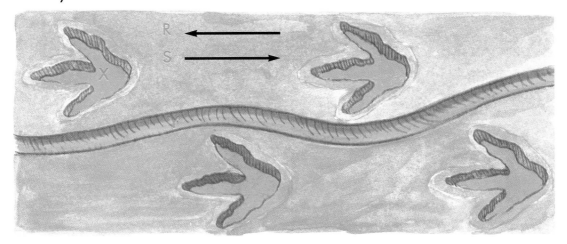

20. Which object is the hottest?
21. What is the temperature of that object?
22. Which object is the coldest?
23. What is the temperature of that object?

A

45 degrees

B

30 degrees

C

60 degrees

85

A

1	2	3
1. cough	1. remains	1. lying
2. pour	2. shriek	2. laying
3. volcano	3. reason	3. breathe
4. neither	4. attract	4. breath
5. adventure	5. safety	5. pacing
6. supplies	6. strangely	6. packing
	7. untangle	

B

Looking for Carla

Carla was not in sight. That meant that Carla was still back there in the jungle. Edna took a couple of steps into the jungle. She stopped and looked down the path. She couldn't see anything. Part of her mind told her, "Don't go back there. You'll get killed." Then another part of her mind said, "You've got to help Carla. Go back."

Edna thought of calling to Carla. But then she thought that the sound of her voice might attract the monster.

Suddenly, she noticed that she was walking back toward the clearing. She had decided to try to help her friend.

She crouched over and kept near the side of the path. She was ready to duck behind a tree as soon as she spotted Tyrannosaurus. She couldn't hear anything except her breath and the sounds of her feet moving through the green plants. Step, step, step—she moved down the path.

She noticed a beautiful flower growing in the middle of the path. She noticed that the birds in the jungle were not squawking. "I wonder why they are silent?" she asked herself.

She answered, "They probably flew away when Tyrannosaurus ran into the clearing."

Then once again she noticed how quiet it was. Step, step, step.

Edna was nearly all the way back to the clearing when she heard Tyrannosaurus. She could smell the dinosaur, too, but she couldn't see it. Edna ducked behind a tree on the side of the path. Now her mind started to think about the things that might have happened.

Maybe Tyrannosaurus had already found Carla and maybe Tyrannosaurus . . . "No," she told herself. "Don't think about things like that. Carla is all right."

Edna stayed behind the tree for a minute or two. Tyrannosaurus didn't seem to be moving toward her. So slowly she snuck back onto the path and moved toward the sound of the breathing. Closer and closer. Then she saw Carla lying near the path. Her leg was tangled up in some vines. She was lying very still.

Part of Edna's mind said this: "Carla is not moving, so she is dead."

Another part of Edna's mind said this: "No. She is not dead and she is not hurt. She is lying very still because

Tyrannosaurus is very near and she doesn't want to move." Edna snuck up a little closer. Now she could see Tyrannosaurus. The dinosaur was at the edge of the clearing, looking in the direction of Carla. But the dinosaur was not standing still. It was pacing and turning its head from one side to another, as if it was looking for something.

Edna looked at Carla. She was all right.

On the far end of the clearing were the remains of the flying dinosaur. For some reason, Tyrannosaurus was not eating them.

Suddenly, Edna got an idea of how to save Carla. The plan was very dangerous, but Edna felt strangely brave. She felt that she had to try to help Carla. Edna's plan was to catch the dinosaur's attention. She would go into the jungle and make a lot of noise. Tyrannosaurus would come after the noise. When the dinosaur followed the noise, Carla would be able to free herself and run to safety.

Edna's heart was pounding. She knew that she would have to be very fast. She remembered how fast Tyrannosaurus moved through the jungle.

Suddenly, Tyrannosaurus turned around. Three Triceratops dinosaurs came into the clearing. They held their heads down as they moved toward Tyrannosaurus. Tyrannosaurus ran toward them and then stopped. It opened its mouth very wide and let out a terrible shriek.

"Now," Edna told herself. She ran toward Carla, who was already sitting up and trying to untangle her leg.

Edna grabbed the vines and tried to pull them free. It seemed to take forever. Carla didn't say anything. The girls tugged at the vines and tried to get Carla's leg free. The dinosaurs were very close to them.

Number your paper from 1 through 24.

Skill Items

Write the word from the box that means the same thing as the underlined part of each sentence.

armor	shabby	docked	illegal
graph	mast	bailed	sped

1. The sled underline went fast down the hill.
2. Stealing is not legal.
3. The animal's hard covering protects it from enemies.

Use the words in the box to write a complete sentence.

immediately	terribly	moaned	attracted

4. The smell ▇▇▇ flies ▇▇▇.

Review Items

5. What do we call the part of a ship where the cargo is carried?
6. How long ago did dinosaurs live on Earth?
   - 30 thousand years ago
   - 1 million years ago
   - 100 million years ago

Write the letter that shows where each place is.

7. Italy
8. Egypt
9. Greece
10. Turkey
11. Spain
12. Land of the Vikings

13. Concord
14. San Francisco
15. Canada
16. United States
17. Mexico

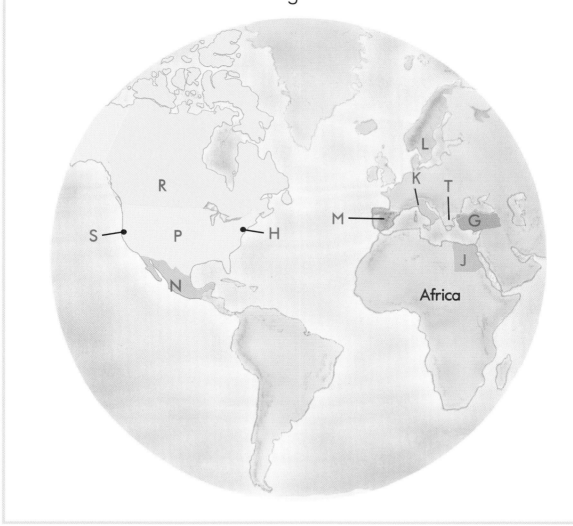

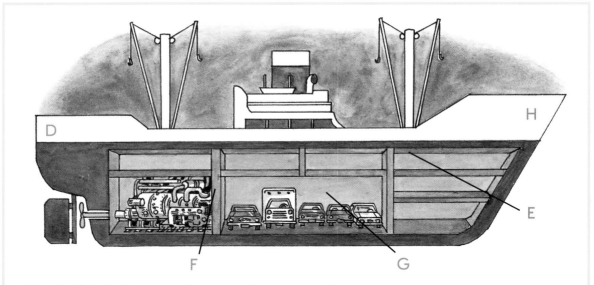

18. Which letter shows the stern?
19. Which letter shows the hold?
20. Which letter shows a deck?
21. Which letter shows the bow?
22. Which letter shows a bulkhead?

23. Lynn is 4 miles high. Fran is 20 miles high. Who is colder?
24. Tell why.

86

A

1	2	3
1. <u>how</u>ever	1. swift	1. quake
2. <u>ex</u>plodes	2. glanced	2. hardened
3. <u>underwater</u>	3. thud	3. explosion
4. <u>v</u>olcano	4. pours	4. prancing
5. <u>coughing</u>		

B Volcanos and Earthquakes

You will be reading about volcanos and earthquakes. A volcano is a mountain that is made of hot melted rock. That rock comes from inside the earth.

The picture shows what a volcano would look like if it were cut in half and we could see the inside.

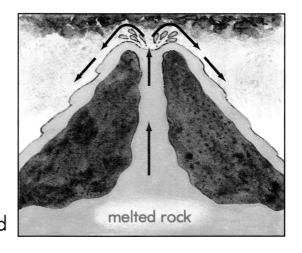

melted rock

There is a layer of melted rock in the earth far below the volcano. The melted rock moves up to the surface of the earth. When the melted rock pours out onto the surface of the earth, the rock cools and becomes hard. More melted rock piles up on top of the hardened rock. The volcano keeps growing in the shape of a cone.

The volcano may pour out great clouds of smoke.

Sometimes a volcano explodes. Sometimes there are earthquakes around volcanos.

C Explosion

Carla and Edna were tugging at the vines that were tangled around Carla's leg. The vines were like thick, sticky ropes that wouldn't let go. Occasionally, Edna glanced up and looked at what was happening in the clearing. The three Triceratops dinosaurs were lined up, waiting for Tyrannosaurus. The giant Tyrannosaurus was prancing around with its mouth wide open. It would move toward the Triceratops dinosaurs and then it would back away. From time to time, it would let out a terrible shriek.

The leg is free! Take her hand and help her up. Now run. Keep an eye on her. Let her run in front of you. Push her on the back so that she runs faster. Is that as fast as she can run? Let's get out of here. Keep running. Look, there's the beach. Run. Right down to the edge of the water. Stop. Turn around. Look back. They're not coming after you. Safe. Safe.

The girls stood near the edge of the water for a few minutes, listening to the sounds that came from the jungle. The sounds told them that a terrible fight was going on. Tyrannosaurus would shriek from time to time. Then there would be a great thud. After a few minutes, the shriek of

Tyrannosaurus turned into a cry. Just then the whole island seemed to shake.

The tops of the trees began to shake. They shook so hard that coconuts fell to the ground. The birds left the island. They were flying to the west. Suddenly the ground shook with such force that Edna fell down. The red beach moved up and then down. It rocked to one side and then to the other.

"Earthquake!" Carla yelled.

Some trees near the edge of the jungle fell over. As Edna sat up, she noticed a great cloud of smoke over the top of the island. "Volcano," she shouted.

The smoke boiled and billowed into the air with great speed. Within a few seconds, it had covered the whole eastern part of the sky. And still the smoke cloud was growing.

"Come on," Edna shouted. She ran toward the boat. The beach suddenly shook. She stumbled, fell, and slid through the red sand. She got up and ran. The sky was now becoming dark, as the enormous cloud continued to grow.

The girls reached the boat and turned it over. They pushed it into the shallow water. Just as they were a few meters from the shore, a terrible quake shook the island. It made a large crack in the sand beach. That crack moved out into the water, right under the boat. Suddenly, Edna noticed that the sand under her feet had disappeared. She slipped underwater. The currents were very swift and she felt her feet being pulled into the current.

Edna reached up and tried to grab on to something. Her hand grabbed a rope that was attached to the front of the boat. She held on to the rope with all her might. The currents were spinning her around, but she kept a ⭐ tight grip on the rope. Slowly she pulled herself up to the boat. She came out of the water coughing.

As soon as she caught her breath, she called, "Carla, Carla!" She had salt water in her eyes, so she couldn't see well.

"I'm here," Carla answered.

Edna rubbed her eyes with one hand and looked in the direction of the voice. Carla was sitting in the boat. She helped Edna get into the boat. The sky was so dark now that it was almost like night.

Suddenly, there was a terrible explosion. The explosion had so much force that it seemed to press the air against Edna's face. This pressing feeling came before the sound of the explosion. The sound was like nothing that Edna had ever heard. It was so loud that her ears rang for hours. That explosion had so much force that it knocked down all the trees on the island.

The girls began to row into the deeper part of the ocean. "Where are we going to go?" Carla asked.

"I don't know," Edna replied. "I don't know." She did know one thing, however. She knew that she didn't want to be near that island.

Skill Items

The rim of the volcano exploded.
1. What word means **made a bang and flew apart?**
2. What word means **a mountain formed from hot flowing rock?**
3. What word means **the top edge** of the volcano?

Review Items
4. How many seconds are in one minute?
5. Some clocks have a hand that counts seconds. When that hand goes all the way around the clock, how much time has passed?
6. The second hand on a clock went around 7 times. How much time passed?
7. In what country are peacocks wild animals?

8. What is the temperature of the water in each jar?
9. Write the letter of each jar that is filled with ocean water.
10. Jar C is filled with ocean water. How do you know?

32 degrees 32 degrees 32 degrees 32 degrees 32 degrees 32 degrees

A   B   C   D   E   F

11. Things closest to the bottom of the pile went into the pile ▓▓▓▓.

12. Write the letter of the layer that went into the pile first.

13. Write the letter of the layer that we live in.

14. Which layer went into the pile later, A or B?

15. Write the letter of the layer where we would find the skeletons of humans.

16. Write the letter of the layer where we find the skeletons of dinosaurs.

17. Write the letter of the layer where we find the skeletons of horses.

18. What's the name of layer C?

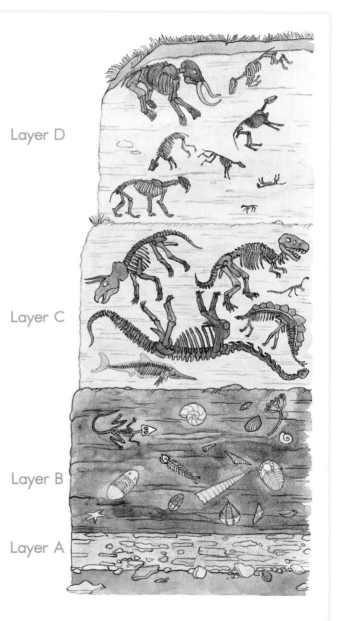

Layer D

Layer C

Layer B

Layer A

Use these names to answer the questions: **Tyrannosaurus, Triceratops.**

19. What is animal R?
20. What is animal S?

21. What are clouds made of?
22. What kind of cloud does the picture show?
23. What happens to a drop at B?

24. The picture shows half a hailstone. How many times did the stone go through a cloud?

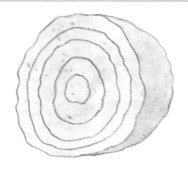

A

1	2	3
1. approach	1. <u>bli</u>sters	1. throat
2. bandage	2. <u>a</u>dventure	2. chew
3. laundry	3. <u>un</u>real	3. nor
4. stomach	4. <u>nei</u>ther	4. rim
5. mysterious	5. <u>sha</u>dow	5. beneath
6. Tuesday	6. <u>supp</u>lies	

B

Back in the Lifeboat

The lifeboat was floating on a bright, shining sea. The sea was so calm that it looked almost as if it was made of glass. When Edna looked down, she could see different colors. Where the water was not very deep, the color was green. Deeper spots were blue, with the deepest spots dark blue. The sun pounded down on the girls. Edna had blisters on her hands from rowing, but she was not rowing now. She was just sitting. In the far distance, a billowing cloud rose high into the sky. Edna could no longer see the island.

As she sat there in the lifeboat, she realized that they didn't have supplies. There were no other islands in sight.

The boat seemed to be drifting in a current, and the current was taking the boat to the west. But how long would it be before the girls spotted another island? What would they do if they didn't find land soon? Edna was already starting to feel thirsty. She tried not to think about it, but when she swallowed, she noticed that her throat was dry.

Neither Edna nor Carla had said anything for a long time. The adventure they had on the island was so unreal that Edna didn't know what to say.

Suddenly, Edna noticed that the boat was drifting faster. When she looked to the west, she got a very sick feeling. In the distance, she could see the rim of a whirlpool.

The boat was moving toward it, speeding faster and faster, through the green water.

The rushing sounds got louder and louder. Now the boat was moving over the rim of the whirlpool. "Hang on," Edna shouted, as she grabbed on to the side of the boat. She hung on with all her might. The boat sped around and around and around. Edna looked up at the sky. The clouds seemed to be spinning around and around. The boat was going deeper and deeper into the whirlpool.

Now Edna could see a great cone of water above the boat. The boat was spinning so fast that its force pressed Edna against the bottom of the boat. She felt sick and dizzy. She squeezed her eyes closed as tightly as she could. Then the sounds seemed to fade away and everything went dark.

• • •

Heat. Terrible heat. "Where am I?" Edna said aloud. Then she realized that she was lying in the bottom of the lifeboat. The sun was beating down on her face. The boat was not moving. As she sat up, she realized that there was some water in the bottom of the boat. The water was very warm.

Edna looked over at Carla. "Are you okay?" Edna asked.

Carla looked very sick. "I think so," she said. "What happened?"

"I don't know," Edna answered. "We were in a whirlpool. That's the last thing I remember. Are we dead?"

"I don't think we're dead," Carla replied. "But I don't remember how we got out of the whirlpool. I passed out."

"I passed out, too," Edna said. Slowly, she turned around and looked at the ocean. It was perfectly calm. She didn't see any signs of whirlpools. And she didn't see any billowing clouds that marked the island. "We must be far from the island," Edna said.

Edna looked over the side of the boat, into the water. It was very dark blue. She could see some fish swimming around beneath the boat. They seemed to like staying in the shadow of the boat. As Edna looked at the fish, she remembered something she had once read. Fish have a lot of fresh water in them. If you chew on raw fish, you can squeeze the water out. Edna didn't like the idea of chewing on raw fish, but she knew that without water, she and Carla would not last for more than a few more hours in the hot sun.

Number your paper from 1 through 23.

Skill Items

Write the word or words from the box that mean the same thing as the underlined part of each sentence.

shriek	breath	surface	armor
skeletons	an instant	a sense	tangle

1. The animal <u>bones</u> were near the big old tree.
2. He was afraid for <u>a moment</u>.
3. The <u>top layer</u> of the lake was as smooth as glass.

Use the words in the box to write complete sentences.

volcano	practiced	attracted	exploded
	sense	immediately	strangely

4. The smell ▆▆ flies ▆▆.
5. The rim of the ▆▆ ▆▆.

Review Items
6. Which direction would you go to get from the main part of the United States to Canada?
7. Which country is **smaller,** Canada or the United States?
8. Where do **fewer** people live, in Canada or in the United States?

9. Which country is **warmer,** Canada or the United States?
10. Write the letters of the 3 things you find in the Bermuda Triangle.

      a. huge waves   d. whirlpools

      b. mountains   e. icebergs

      c. streams   f. sudden storms

11. Write the letter of the footprint made by the heaviest animal.
12. Write the letter of the footprint made by the lightest animal.

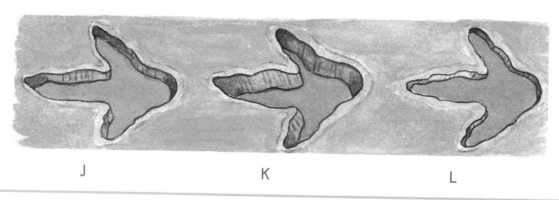

J   K   L

13. How long ago did dinosaurs live on Earth?
    - 10 million years ago
    - 100 million years ago
    - 100 thousand years ago
14. Two things happen to melted rock when it moves down the sides of a volcano. Name those 2 things.
15. What is it called when the earth shakes and cracks?
16. Is the world **round** or **flat?**
17. Did Columbus think that the world was **round** or **flat?**

18. Who sailed across the ocean first, the Vikings or Columbus?
19. Who was the first president of the United States?
20. Who is the president of the United States today?

21. What is the temperature of the water in each jar?
22. Write the letter of each jar that is filled with ocean water.
23. Jar B is filled with ocean water. How do you know?

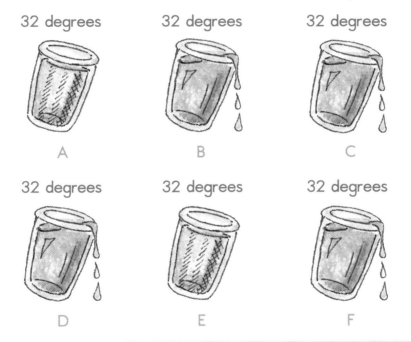

32 degrees
A

32 degrees
B

32 degrees
C

32 degrees
D

32 degrees
E

32 degrees
F

88

A

1
1. actually
2. exhibit
3. museum
4. Leonard
5. character
6. embarrassed

2
1. underwater
2. overboard
3. somehow
4. handful

3
1. directed
2. divided
3. bandages
4. approached
5. sandwiches
6. honestly

4
1. Monday
2. laundry
3. yesterday
4. mysterious
5. stomach
6. Tuesday

B

Saved

Edna realized that she and Carla needed water. Without it, they would not last for more than a few more hours. Edna moved to the front of the boat and started to look for fishing gear. But then she noticed a slim line of smoke in the distance. It wasn't the billowing smoke that came from the island. "A ship," Edna said as she stood up.

"I think there's a ship over there." She pointed.

Carla stood up. "You're right. I can see it, and I think it's coming in this direction."

The next hour seemed longer than any hour Edna ever remembered. Edna didn't do anything but watch the approaching ship. She felt that if she stopped watching it, it would disappear. As it got closer, she recognized the ship. "That's Dad's ship," she shouted. "They're coming back for us."

•　　　•　　　•

The crew members helped Edna and Carla onto the deck of the ship. Captain Parker put his arms around the girls. Then Edna started to cry. She didn't want to cry. During the whole adventure, she hadn't cried. But now, as her dad hugged her, she couldn't help it. Tears started to run down her cheeks. "Dad," she said. She was so glad to be back, and she was ashamed for not paying attention to what her father had said.

"I'm glad we found you," Captain Parker said. "Now let's get you taken care of."

Both girls had blisters on their hands from rowing. They were both badly sunburned. And they were very hungry and thirsty. But within an hour, they were fixed up. Now the girls had burn cream on their noses. They had little bandages on their hands. And they had full stomachs. Edna drank three glasses of juice. She ate two sandwiches. And she almost finished a huge piece of pie. But she couldn't make it through that pie. She pushed herself away from the table and stood up. "I'm full," she said.

"I'd like to talk with you girls," Captain Parker said. The girls followed him to the map room. Captain Parker told them to sit down. "All right," he said. "What happened?"

"I know we shouldn't have been playing around with the lifeboat," Carla said. "But I'm the one to blame. Edna didn't want to do it. It was my idea."

"Just tell me what happened," Captain Parker said. So the girls told the whole story: how the boat fell into the water, how they got sucked into the whirlpool, how they found the mysterious island, and what happened on the island. After the girls had finished telling about the second whirlpool, Carla said, "I don't know how we got out of the whirlpool, but we did, somehow. Then the next thing we knew, your ship was coming back toward us."

"That's some story," Captain Parker said. "Do you honestly think all those things happened?"

"Oh yeah," Edna said. "We're not making it up. It really happened, the whole thing."

Then Carla said, "Don't you believe us?"

Captain Parker smiled. "From the way you tell the story, I think you believe it. But I'm not sure it really happened that way."

"It did happen, Dad," Edna said. "It really did. Everything we told you is true."

"Well then, tell me this," Captain Parker said. "What day of the week was it when you went overboard?"

"Monday," Edna said.

"And you ⭐ spent a night on the island. Is that correct?"

"Yes," Edna agreed.

Captain Parker said, "So what day would that make today?"

"Today is Tuesday," Edna said.

Captain Parker opened the door to the map room and said to a crew member, "Tell these girls what day today is."

The man looked a little puzzled. "Monday," he said.

"Monday?" Edna said. "No, that was yesterday. Today is Tuesday."

The young crew member smiled and said, "What is this, some kind of joke?"

Captain Parker said, "No, everything is all right. Thank you."

Carla said to Edna, "It can't be Monday."

"But it is Monday," Captain Parker said. "You may have had too much sun out there. But it has only been five hours since you left the ship."

"But it really happened, Dad," Edna said.

Later that afternoon, Edna was taking her wet clothes to the laundry room. As she approached the laundry room, she checked the pockets of her pants. She turned one pocket inside out and suddenly she stopped. About a handful of wet red sand fell onto the deck of the ship. If the adventure hadn't happened, how did that sand get into her pocket?

Edna never found the answer to that question.

Number your paper from 1 through 21.

Skill Items

Here are three events that happened in the story.
Write **beginning, middle,** or **end** for each event.
1. In the distance was a slim line of smoke.
2. Captain Parker opened the door to the map room and talked to one of the crew members.
3. Later that afternoon, Edna was taking her wet clothes to the laundry room.

The new exhibit displayed mysterious fish.

4. What word describes things we don't understand?
5. What word means **an arrangement of things for people to look at?**
6. What word means **showed?**

Review Items

7. Who is the president of the United States today?
8. Who was the first president of the United States?

9. When the United States announced that it was a country, England went to war with the United States. Who was the leader of the United States army during the war?
10. Which country won the war?
11. Which country was winning that war in 1777?

12. If you go east from Australia, what ocean do you go through?
13. Captain Parker's ship passed through a place where hundreds of ships have sunk or been lost. Name that place.
14. Two things happen to melted rock when it moves down the sides of a volcano. Name those 2 things.

15. Write the letters of the 5 names that tell about time.
16. Write the letters of the 6 names that tell about distance or length.
17. Write the letter of the name that tells about temperature.
18. Write the letters of the 2 names that tell about speed.

a. meters
b. minutes
c. miles per year
d. hours
e. feet

f. degrees
g. weeks
h. miles
i. inches per hour
j. days

k. inches
l. years
m. centimeters
n. yards

19. The picture shows marks left by an animal. Which arrow shows the direction the animal is moving?
20. Write the letter of the part that shows the mark left by the animal's tail.
21. Write the letter of the part that shows a footprint.

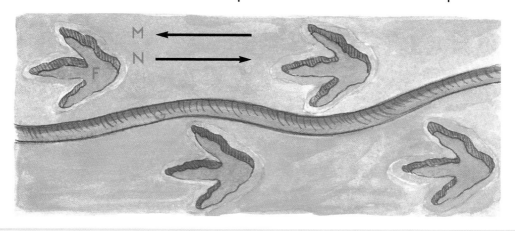

═══ END OF LESSON 88 INDEPENDENT WORK ═══

SPECIAL PROJECT

For today's lesson, you will do a project on dinosaurs. You will make a wall chart that shows some of the great dinosaurs.

Dinosaurs lived during the Mesozoic. The Mesozoic was divided into three parts: The early Mesozoic, the middle Mesozoic, and the late Mesozoic. Tyrannosaurus lived in the late Mesozoic.

Make your chart in three layers. In the bottom layer, show pictures of some dinosaurs that lived in the early Mesozoic. Try to find at least two dinosaurs from the early Mesozoic. Write facts about the dinosaurs that you show on your chart. Tell each dinosaur's name, what it ate, and how big it was.

Do the same thing for the dinosaurs of the middle Mesozoic. Find at least four dinosaurs. One of them may be Apatosaurus, which was much, much bigger than Tyrannosaurus or Triceratops. Put their pictures in the middle layer of the chart. Write facts that tell their names, what they ate, and how big they were.

Do the same thing for the dinosaurs of the late Mesozoic. Find facts and pictures for at least four dinosaurs.

89

A

1
1. arrange
2. magazine
3. material
4. Esther
5. electricity
6. expression

2
1. possible
2. everyone
3. grandmother
4. automobile
5. display
6. exhibit

3
1. embarrassed
2. darted
3. actually
4. hurrying
5. outing
6. pencils

4
1. pace
2. character
3. Leonard
4. museum
5. speech

B

Inventing

Today's story tells about inventing things. You've already read about inventing.

Remember, when somebody makes an object for the first time, the person invents that object.

What did the person who made the first pencil do?

What did the person who made the first light bulb do?

The person who invents the object is called the inventor. And the object is called the invention.

At one time, there were no electric light bulbs. Somebody invented one. That invention showed other people how to make light bulbs.

C ## Grandmother Esther

The year was 1980. Leonard was 12 years old. He was at the museum with his grandmother. Going places with Grandmother Esther was fun, but it was also embarrassing. It was embarrassing because Grandmother Esther had a lot to say, and she talked in a very loud voice. She talked the loudest and the longest about inventing. So when Leonard went to the museum with Grandmother Esther, he was ready to hear a lot of loud talk about inventing.

In the museum, they spent a little time looking at the displays of wild animals and the dinosaurs. Leonard wanted to spend more time here, but Grandmother Esther kept hurrying Leonard along. She would say, "Let's keep moving or we won't see all the things we want to look at in the other parts of the museum."

Leonard knew what parts of the museum his grandmother was talking about—the displays of the first automobiles, the first airplanes, the first computers, and other things, such as the first radios.

So Grandmother Esther swept Leonard through the

display of Egypt 4 thousand years ago. She darted through the exhibit of the cave people and through the display of horses. She slowed her pace as the two approached the display of the first airplanes.

As they walked through the large doorway of the exhibit hall, she announced, "Here is where we see the work of the most important people in the world—the inventors."

Leonard listened to his grandmother's speech about inventors. He nodded and very quietly said, "Yes." He was hoping that she might talk more softly if he talked softly, so he spoke in a voice that was almost a whisper. But it didn't work. Grandmother Esther's voice echoed across the large display hall.

"Without inventors there would be nothing," she said. Other people were starting to look at her and Leonard. Leonard could feel his ears getting hot from embarrassment.

"Where would we be today without inventors?" she asked herself loudly. Then she answered her own question: "We would have no planes because nobody would invent them. We would have no electric lights, no radios. We would not be able to build buildings like this one. We would still be living in <u>caves</u>!"

Grandmother Esther said the word **caves** so loudly that a guard at the other end of the exhibit hall turned around and stared at her. She marched to the display of the first airplane and pointed to it. "This was a great invention," she announced. "The two men who invented it knew that a machine could fly through the air. But other people didn't believe them. They said the inventors were <u>crazy</u> for working 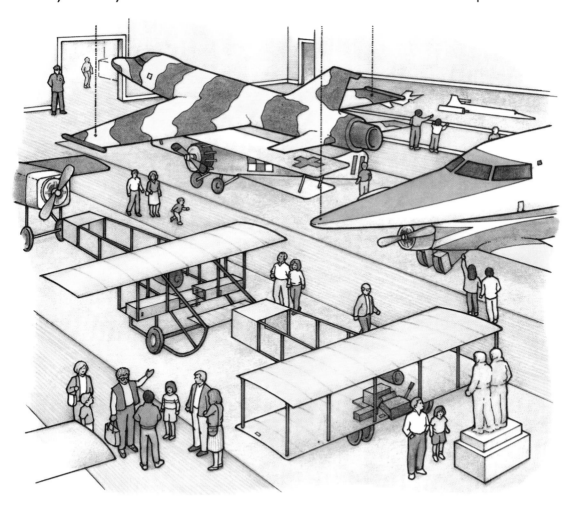 on a flying machine. But the inventors didn't give up. They invented a machine that actually flew. Once others saw that it was possible for machines to fly, they began inventing better flying machines. They invented faster machines and bigger machines. <u>Look</u> at them!" She waved her arm in the direction of the other airplanes on display. Nearly everyone in the hall looked at the rows of planes.

Grandmother Esther marched down the center aisle of the display. In a great voice, she said, "But none of these later planes would be possible without the first one. And the first one would not have been possible without the inventors—those brave men who didn't listen to other people but who knew that we don't have to stay with our feet on the ground. We can <u>fly</u> with the <u>birds</u>!"

The sound of her voice echoed through the hall. Then, one of the people who had been listening to her began to clap. Then others clapped. Soon there was a loud sound of clapping. Even the guard was clapping. Leonard was very embarrassed, but he didn't want to be the only one not clapping. So he clapped, too. He said to himself, "My grandmother is a real character."

Skill Items

Write the word from the box that means the same thing as the underlined part of each sentence.

adventure	enormous	however	swift
approached	displayed	mysterious	glanced

1. The lion was <u>very fast</u>.
2. He went to school, <u>but</u> he was sick.
3. She <u>looked quickly</u> at the sign.

Use the words in the box to write complete sentences.

displayed	adventure	exploded	reason
rim	glanced	mysterious	directed

4. The ▇▇ of the volcano ▇▇.
5. The new exhibit ▇▇ ▇▇ fish.

Review Items

6. How many legs does an insect have?
7. How many legs does a fly have?
8. How many legs does a bee have?
9. How many legs does a spider have?
10. How many parts does a spider's body have?
11. How many parts does a fly's body have?

12. Write the letters of 3 things that were true of humans 40 thousand years ago.
    a. They lived in caves.
    b. They were shorter than people of today.
    c. They were taller than people of today.
    d. They wore animal skins.
    e. They wore hats.
    f. They rode bikes.
    g. They drove cars.

13. Two things happen to melted rock when it moves down the sides of a volcano. Name those 2 things.
14. What is it called when the earth shakes and cracks?
15. If you go west from the United States, what ocean do you go through?
16. What is a baby kangaroo called?
17. What is a group of kangaroos called?

18. Where does a baby kangaroo live right after it is born?
19. How long does it live there?

20. What's the name of the large, beautiful bird of India with a colorful tail?
21. How many meters long is that bird from its head to the end of its tail?

Number your paper from 1 through 21.

1. Write the letter of the footprint made by the lightest animal.
2. Write the letter of the footprint made by the heaviest animal.

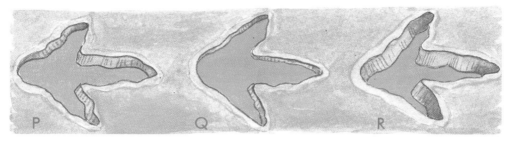

3. The picture shows marks left by an animal. Which arrow shows the direction the animal is moving?
4. Write the letter of the part that shows a footprint.
5. Write the letter of the part that shows the mark left by the animal's tail.

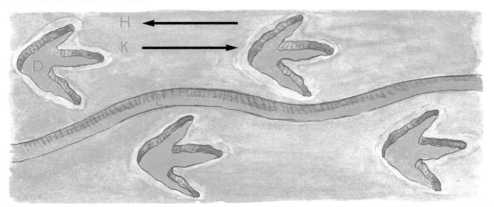

6. How long ago did dinosaurs live on Earth?

7. Each picture has 2 arrows that show how the melted rock moves. Write the letter of the picture that shows 2 correct arrows.

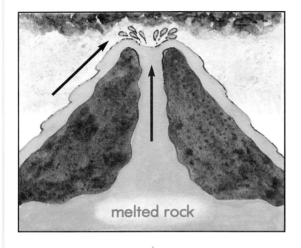

A

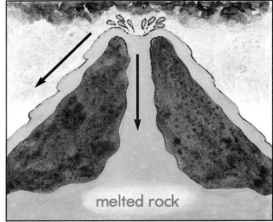

B

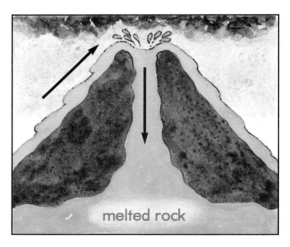

C

D

8. Two things happen to melted rock when it moves down the sides of a volcano. Name those 2 things.
9. What is it called when the earth shakes and cracks?

10. What is a person doing when the person makes an object for the first time?
11. The person who makes an object for the first time is called an ____.
12. The object the person makes is called an ____.

13. Write the letters of the 5 names that tell about time.
14. Write the letters of the 6 names that tell about length or distance.
15. Write the letter of the one name that tells about temperature.
16. Write the letter of the 3 names that tell about speed.

a. miles per hour
b. miles
c. hours
d. meters
e. centimeters per second
f. weeks
g. yards
h. days
i. degrees
j. minutes
k. inches
l. feet
m. years
n. yards per minute
o. centimeters

For each item, write the underlined word or words from the sentences in the box.

> The smell <u>attracted</u> flies <u>immediately</u>.
> The <u>rim</u> of the <u>volcano</u> <u>exploded</u>.
> The new <u>exhibit</u> <u>displayed</u> <u>mysterious</u> fish.

17. What underlining means **showed**?
18. What underlining refers to a mountain formed from hot flowing rock?
19. What underlining means **right now**?
20. What underlining describes things we don't understand?
21. What underlining means the **top edge**?

 END OF TEST 9

A

1
1. <u>sharp</u>-minded
2. <u>ex</u>hibit
3. <u>hard</u>-boiled
4. <u>my</u>self

2
1. <u>out</u>doors
2. <u>rail</u>road
3. <u>stair</u>way
4. <u>under</u>stand

3
1. arranged
2. crazier
3. choked
4. stuffed
5. coughed

4
1. material
2. electricity
3. magazine
4. expression
5. invention
6. inventors

B ## Grandmother Esther's Inventions

Leonard and his grandmother had been in the museum all morning. Now they were sitting outdoors, on the wide stairway that led from the museum. Grandmother Esther was pulling things from her lunch bag and setting them on the stair. And she was still talking. Leonard thought that she would never stop.

"Yes," she said, "I was an inventor myself." Leonard had

heard this story many times. He could say the whole thing as well as she could.

"Yes," she repeated. "But things were different back then. Nobody wanted to listen to a woman inventor. Everybody used to think that inventors were a crazy bunch anyhow. But they thought that a <u>woman</u> inventor had to be even crazier than the other inventors. So nobody listened to me. And so some great inventions were never made."

She took a bite from a hard-boiled egg. Leonard thought she might stop talking while she ate, but she talked with her mouth full. "Yes," she said. "I actually invented the first water bed years before anybody else did. But you couldn't get good material back then. So it leaked a little bit, and everybody said it was a crazy idea."

She continued, "I also invented the folding bicycle. You could fold it up and carry it with you. Just because there were a few little problems with it, people thought it was crazy. But I could have fixed those problems. With just a little more work, I could have made a bike that wouldn't fold up when you were riding it."

Leonard wanted to invent things, too. But what could he invent? Almost without thinking, he said, "Well, the trouble with being an inventor is that everything has already been invented."

☾ Grandmother Esther started to cough. While she was still coughing, she said, "Leonard, what kind of talk is that?" She pointed to the large hall behind her. "Think of how the world looked to people a hundred years ago. They said, 'We've got horse carts and buildings. We have railroads and ships. We must have everything. There is nothing more to invent.' But a few sharp-minded people could see that people <u>didn't</u> have everything."

Leonard realized that she was right. The people who lived in caves thought that everything had been invented. They didn't know about radios and automobiles and planes and leather shoes.

Grandmother Esther was still talking as she ate her sandwich. "The inventor sees things that are not there yet. The inventor thinks about how things could be. Everybody else just sees things as they are now."

Leonard nodded his head. For a moment he thought about what she said. Then he asked, "But how do you think about things that haven't been invented? What do you do, just think of make-believe things?"

She coughed and then she shouted, "Make-believe? Inventors don't deal in make-believe. They deal in what people <u>need</u>. That's where the invention starts. The ⭐ inventor looks around and notices that people have trouble doing some things. The inventor says, "I see a <u>need</u> that people have." Grandmother Esther stuffed the rest of her sandwich in her mouth. In an instant, she continued talking. "After the inventor sees a need, the inventor figures out how to meet that need."

"I don't understand," Leonard said.

She pointed back toward the exhibit hall and said, "The two men who invented the airplane saw a need. They saw that people could get places faster if they could fly in a straight line rather than going around on roads. They said to themselves, 'Let's make something that will let people go places faster.' So they invented a flying machine."

She continued, "The person who invented the car saw a need. That person saw that horses were a lot of work. People spent a lot of time feeding them and taking care of them. With a car, people would save a lot of time. With a car they could also go faster from place to place."

She pointed her finger at Leonard. "Remember, if you want to be an inventor, start with a need. Then figure out how to meet that need."

C Number your paper from 1 through 21.

Skill Items

She automatically arranged the flowers.

1. What word means **without thinking?**
2. What word means that she put things where she wanted them?

Review Items

3. Write the letters of the things you find in the Bermuda Triangle.

    a. huge waves   c. streams   e. icebergs

    b. mountains   d. whirlpools   f. sudden storms

4. The picture shows half a hailstone. How many times did the stone go through a cloud?

5. What is a person doing when the person makes an object for the first time?
6. The person who makes an object for the first time is called an ▮▮▮.
7. The object the person makes is called an ▮▮▮.

Write **W** for warm-blooded animals and **C** for cold-blooded animals.

8. beetle
9. cow
10. horse
11. spider
12. bee

13. Tom is 4 miles high. Jack is 20 miles high. Who is colder?
14. Tell why.

15. Look at the picture. Jar M is filled with fresh water. Jar P is filled with ocean water. Which jar is heavier?
16. Which jar will freeze at 32 degrees?
17. Will the other jar freeze when it is **more than 32 degrees** or **less than 32 degrees?**

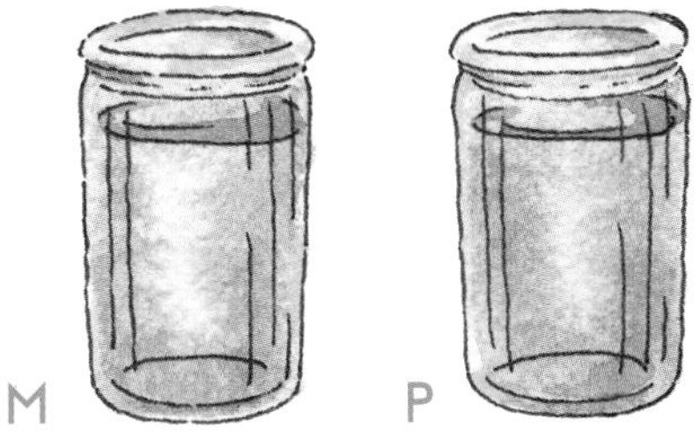

18. Palm trees cannot live in places that get ____.
19. What are the branches of palm trees called?
20. Name 2 things that grow on different palm trees.

Study Item

21. Today's story mentions the two men who invented the first airplane. Look in a book on airplanes, in an encyclopedia, or on a computer and see if you can find out the names of these two men.

A

1	2
1. invisible	1. chuckled
2. suggest	2. ceiling
3. automatically	3. repeated
4. protection	4. magazine
5. vocabulary	5. expression
6. explanation	

B Trying to Discover Needs

Leonard tried to think like an inventor, but the job was a lot harder than Leonard thought it would be. At first, Leonard had a lot of trouble trying to figure out things that people might need. He tried to remember what Grandmother Esther had said. "Start with a need," she had said. "Then figure out how to meet that need." But figuring out what people need was a big problem.

Leonard started out by asking people, "What do you need?" First, he asked his father. "Say, Dad, I'm thinking of inventing some things. What do you need?"

His dad was reading a paper. He looked up at Leonard and smiled.

"Well," his dad said as he put the paper down. "Well," he repeated. "Let me see." He looked up at the ceiling. "Let me see." Leonard's dad chuckled. "I could use more money. Maybe you can invent a tree that grows money."

Leonard smiled. Then he waited.

His dad said, "It would be nice to have less traffic on the road. Maybe you could invent a way to take traffic off the road."

Leonard didn't even smile over his dad's last idea. "Come on, Dad," he said. "I'm not kidding around. I need some ideas about things I might be able to invent. But I have to start with a <u>need</u>."

"Well, let me see," his father said, and looked down at the paper again. "There are probably a lot of things that people need. I just can't think of one right now."

"Okay," Leonard said. "Thanks anyhow." To himself, he was saying, "My dad just doesn't have the mind of an inventor."

Next, Leonard talked to his mother. "Mom," he said, "I need ideas for inventions." He explained his problem to her. She was working at her desk.

"Oh, dear," she said. "Every time I go somewhere I can think of a million things that would make good inventions. Let me see . . . ." She rubbed her chin and looked off into space.

☾ "Let me see," she repeated. "Oh, yes," she said after a few moments. "I would like to have something that automatically made up the grocery list. You know, when the refrigerator gets low on milk, the word **milk** automatically goes on the list. Or when we run out of peanut butter, **peanut butter** goes on the list."

"Yeah," Leonard said. "That sounds pretty good. But how would that work?"

His mother looked at him with a puzzled expression. "Leonard," she said, "I'm not the inventor. You asked if I knew of something that should be invented. You didn't ask me how to invent it. If you want to know how to invent it, go ask your grandmother."

So Leonard asked his grandmother. He first explained his mother's idea. Then he said, "But I don't know how to invent that kind of list."

Grandmother Esther was reading a car magazine. She looked up over her glasses and shook her head no. She said, "Your mother has had that crazy idea about the list for twenty years. She must have tried to get me to invent that list fifty times. And I must have told her five thousand times that I don't know how to invent a list that automatically writes down things when you get low on them. But every time I turn around, here she is again, talking about that same invention. I think your mother's problem is that she hates to go grocery shopping and she doesn't like to make up grocery lists. Now I'm not saying that it's impossible to invent something that would make up lists. I'm just saying that you're looking at one inventor who doesn't know how to do it."

"Okay," Leonard said. "Thanks anyhow." As he left the room, Grandmother Esther was looking at her magazine, talking to herself. She was saying, "Again and again and again I kept telling her, I don't know how to do it. But she kept coming back with the same idea, that stupid list writer."

During the week that followed, Leonard talked to nearly everybody about things they thought should be invented. At the end of the week, he didn't have any good ideas for inventions. But he had discovered something. People just don't seem to be very good at telling about things that they need. Leonard said to himself, "Maybe the hardest part of being an inventor is finding something to invent."

C Number your paper from 1 through 24.

Skill Items

Use the words in the box to write complete sentences.

actually	exhibit	directed	automatically
character	displayed	divided	arranged

1. The new ___ ___ mysterious fish.
2. She ___ ___ the flowers.

Review Items

3. A force is a ___.

4. Which picture shows the largest force?
5. Which picture shows the smallest force?

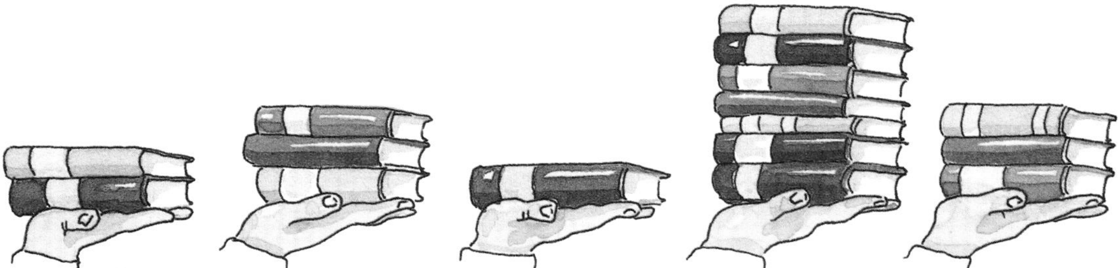

A B C D E

6. The men who invented the first airplane saw a need. What need?
7. Who sailed across the ocean first, the Vikings or Columbus?

Write the letter that shows where each place is.

8. Italy
9. Egypt
10. Greece
11. Turkey
12. Spain
13. Land of the Vikings

14. Concord
15. San Francisco
16. Canada
17. United States
18. Mexico

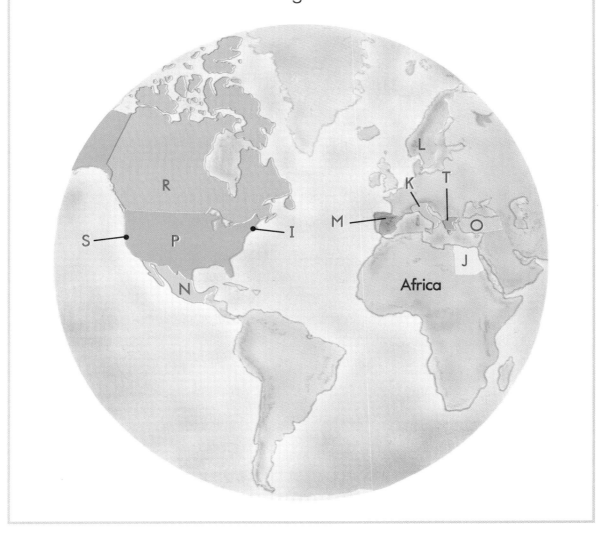

19. Write the letter of the footprint made by the heaviest animal.
20. Write the letter of the footprint made by the lightest animal.

The picture shows marks left by an animal.
21. Which arrow shows the direction the animal is moving?
22. Write the letter of the part that shows a footprint.
23. Write the letter of the part that shows the mark left by the animal's tail.

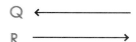

Study Item
24. The two-wheeled bicycle is not very old. It was probably hard for somebody to get the idea of a two-wheeled bicycle because it seemed impossible for somebody to move along on two wheels without falling over. Find out when J. K. Starley invented his two-wheeled *Ariel* bicycle.

A

1	2	3
1. assignment	1. <u>check</u>er	1. Frank
2. solution	2. <u>mudd</u>y	2. mess
3. arithmetic	3. <u>peda</u>l	3. Rita
4. empty	4. <u>sub</u>tract	4. Sarah
5. electricity	5. <u>in</u>visible	5. towels
		6. suggested

B

Bad Ideas

Leonard had tried asking people about things that they thought he could invent. But the people he asked weren't very good about giving him good ideas. One of Leonard's friends, Frank, suggested inventing a vacation that lasted all year long. Another friend, Teddy, wanted a machine that made ice cream from dirt. Ann wanted something to put on her teeth so she would never have to brush them.

Rita wanted a pair of wings so she could fly. Sarah wanted something that would make her invisible. Freddie wanted a bicycle that you didn't have to pedal. You'd just sit on the thing and it would take you places. All these people had ideas about things that they wanted, but most of these ideas were dreams.

"Dreams are a problem," Grandmother Esther told Leonard. He had just told her that he was thinking about giving up the idea of being an inventor. And he had told her why. "Yes, dreams are a problem," she repeated. "Here's why, young man. There are dreams that are wishes. And there are dreams that an inventor has. The line between these dreams is not always clear." Grandmother Esther continued, "Think of the men who invented the first plane. They had a dream, a crazy dream. They wanted to fly. Men with legs who had stood on the ground from the time they were born wanted to fly with the birds. That was a dream as crazy as the dream of becoming invisible or the dream of a bicycle that you don't have to pedal. And I can't help you out. You'll have to find out which dreams are just empty wishes and which dreams may turn into inventions."

"Okay," Leonard said and left the room.

☾ Grandmother Esther was talking to herself about dreams. "Where would we be without dreams? The inventor must have them. And who is to say that a dream is crazy? It was a crazy dream to have lights that ran by electricity or machines that could add and subtract. It was a crazy dream to . . ."

Leonard was ready to forget about being an inventor. But then something happened that changed the way he looked at the problem. As he walked into the kitchen, he noticed that he had mud on the bottom of his shoes. He hadn't noticed it before. Now it was too late. He had made tracks all over the house. If only he had noticed that his shoes were dirty. For a moment, he felt very dumb for tracking mud all over the house. He could almost hear what his mother was going to say: "You should always check your shoes before coming into the house."

Leonard tiptoed over to the outside door and took off his muddy shoes. He got some paper towels and started to clean up the mess. Then, when he had almost cleaned the last footprint on the kitchen floor, an idea hit him. It ★ hit him so hard that it put a smile on his face. Just like that, he knew how to think like an inventor. He said out loud, "I need a shoe checker. I know I need it because when I don't have one, I don't do a good job of checking my feet."

A shoe checker wasn't a bad idea for an invention. But the idea wasn't the most important thing to Leonard. The way he got the idea was the important thing. He didn't do something well. Then he figured out that he needed something to help him do it well.

That's how to figure out things to invent. You don't ask people. You do things. And when you do them, you pay attention to problems that you have. Each of the problems that you have tells you about something that you could invent to solve the problem.

Leonard's mother walked into the kitchen and saw Leonard smiling. "This is the first time I've seen you have a good time while you clean up a mess," she said.

"That's because I like this mess," Leonard said.

His mother shook her head. "He must take after his grandmother," she said to herself.

Number your paper from 1 through 25.

Skill Items

Here are three events that happened in the story.
Write **beginning, middle,** or **end** for each event.
1. Leonard's mother walked into the kitchen and saw Leonard smiling.
2. Grandmother Esther was talking to herself about dreams.
3. One of Leonard's friends, Frank, suggested inventing a vacation that lasted all year long.

They were impressed by her large vocabulary.
4. What word means they thought her vocabulary was very good?
5. What word refers to all the words a person knows?

Review Items

6. Three thousand years ago, part of Greece went to war with ▉▉▉.
7. The war began because a queen from ▉▉▉ ran away with a man from ▉▉▉.
8. ▉▉▉ ships went to war with Troy.
   • 1 hundred   • 1 thousand   • 5 thousand
9. How long did the war last?

Write the time for each event shown on the time line.

10. Eric and Tom were in the city of the future.

11. The year Thrig was from

12. Now

13. You were born.

14. Eric and Tom were in San Francisco.

15. The United States became a country.

16. Columbus discovered America.

17. Eric and Tom were in the Land of the Vikings.

18. Eric and Tom were in Egypt.

19. Eric and Tom saw a saber-toothed tiger.

20. The first thing you do when you think like an inventor is find a ▬.
21. What's the next thing you do?

22. When the United States announced that it was a country, England went to war with the United States. Who was the leader of the United States army during the war?
23. Which country won the war?
24. Which country was winning that war in 1777?

25. How many seconds are in one minute?

A

1
1. example
2. energy
3. device
4. respond

2
1. <u>when</u>ever
2. <u>shop</u>keeper
3. <u>ear</u>muffs
4. <u>bed</u>time
5. <u>bath</u>tub

3
1. impressed
2. forgetting
3. explanation
4. buzzer
5. automatically

4
1. mentioned
2. sternly
3. matching
4. protection
5. unfolded
6. bakery

5
1. collar
2. difficult
3. hood
4. plastic
5. raise
6. vocabulary

B

A Plan for Inventing

Thinking like an inventor was difficult for Leonard until he figured out this plan: He did different things. And he noticed each time he had a problem. When he noticed a problem, he knew that he had a <u>need</u>. He needed something that would solve that problem. The thing he needed to solve the problem was an invention.

After Leonard worked out his plan for finding needs, he

tried to do all kinds of things. He washed the car, washed the windows, and washed the dog. He washed the floors and the walls and the dishes. He helped his dad fix a table. He helped the man who lived next door change a tire on his car.

All the time Leonard did these things, his mind was working. He tried to see where he had problems. For three weeks he did things and noticed the problems that he had. And at the end of three weeks, he had a big list of things that he might invent. Some of the ideas were pretty good.

Leonard had found out that he wasn't very good at cracking raw eggs, and he thought of an invention that would crack egg shells. Leonard had found out that he was always forgetting to hang up his clothes when he took them off at night. Then his mother would come in and say, "Leonard, Leonard, look at your clothes, all over the place." Leonard figured out that what he needed was a tape that would come on just before bedtime. The voice on the tape would say, "Leonard, Leonard, hang up your clothes. Don't just drop them under your nose."

Leonard had a problem each time it rained. Leonard hated umbrellas, so he never took one with him. But then he would be caught in the rain without an umbrella. He would get soaked.

He thought of a way to meet his need for some protection from the rain. Why not invent a coat that has a special hood? When the hood is not being used, it looks like a big collar. But when the hood is unfolded, it becomes a little umbrella.

Leonard discovered that he had a great problem when he tried to wash his dog. The problem was that Leonard got all wet. If he tried to wash the dog in the bathtub, the dog would jump out in the middle of the bath and shake. The room would then be covered with water. Leonard would then have to spend a lot of time cleaning up the mess. If Leonard washed the dog outside, the problem was not as great, but Leonard still got soaked.

He thought of an invention to meet this need. The invention was a large plastic box with holes in it. First you would fill a tub with water. Then you'd put the dog in the tub. Next, you'd put the plastic box over the tub. The dog would stick its head out through one of the holes. You could reach through the other holes and wash the dog and you wouldn't get wet while you were washing the dog. "Not bad," Leonard said to himself when he got this idea. "Not bad at all."

Leonard made pictures of some of his ideas. He showed them to the members of his family and he explained how they worked. His father said, "Leonard, I'm impressed."

Leonard's mother said, "Leonard, those are very good ideas. But did you ever think of inventing a machine that would automatically write out the things that you need at the grocery store?"

When Leonard's mother mentioned the list-making machine, Grandmother Esther said, "Stop talking about that crazy invention. Leonard seems to have some good ideas here. They show that the boy has been thinking like an inventor. Now he needs to stop thinking and start inventing." She looked sternly at Leonard.

Leonard smiled and said, "But I still don't know which thing I should invent."

"They're all pretty good," his father said.

His mother said, "I like the machine that makes up a list of things to buy."

Leonard said, "I'm not sure I've found the right idea yet."

Leonard shook his head. He was becoming very tired of trying to be an inventor.

C Number your paper from 1 through 19.

Skill Items

Use the words in the box to write complete sentences.

impressed	arranged	honestly	stuffed
repeated	automatically	stomach	vocabulary

1. She _____ _____ the flowers.
2. They were _____ by her large _____.

Review Items

3. Write the letters of the 6 names that tell about distance or length.
4. Write the letters of the 5 names that tell about time.
5. Write the letters of the 2 names that tell about speed.
6. Write the letter of the one name that tells about temperature.

   a. degrees
   b. minutes
   c. miles
   d. inches
   e. meters per week
   f. years
   g. miles per hour
   h. centimeters
   i. yards
   j. hours
   k. weeks
   l. meters
   m. days
   n. feet

7. How far is it from New York City to San Francisco?
   - 15 hundred miles
   - 25 hundred miles
   - 4 thousand miles

8. All machines make it easier for someone to ▇▇▇.
9. Who was the first president of the United States?
10. Who is the president of the United States today?
11. Things closest to the bottom of the pile went into the pile ▇▇▇.

12. What are clouds made of?
13. What kind of cloud does the picture show?
14. What happens to a drop at B?

15. Write the letter of every line that is one inch long.
16. Write the letter of every line that is one centimeter long.

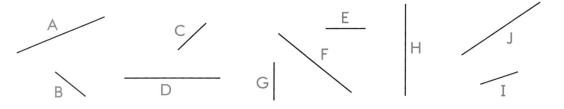

17. What is the name of the country with the arrows?
18. How far is it from **A** to **B**?
19. How far is it from **C** to **D**?

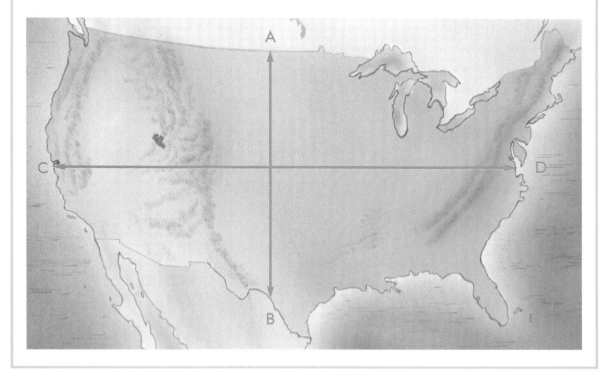

A

1
1. <u>inter</u>est
2. <u>a</u>side
3. <u>Grand</u>ma
4. <u>en</u>ergy

2
1. <u>ex</u>ample
2. <u>ex</u>pect
3. <u>ex</u>cuse
4. <u>cle</u>ver

3
1. counter
2. kneeling
3. blocking
4. traced
5. serves

4
1. beam
2. dance
3. respond
4. she'd
5. target

B

The Electric Eye

Leonard was walking to school. Grandmother Esther was on her way to her exercise class. The exercise class was held near Leonard's school, so she was walking with him. Whenever she walked, she talked, and talked, and talked. And when she talked about inventing, she talked very loudly. Leonard knew that she wasn't shouting at him. He knew that she wasn't mad when she pointed her finger and raised her voice. He knew these things. But the other people who were walking along the street didn't know. They stopped and stared at Grandmother Esther. To them, it must have seemed that she was yelling at Leonard.

Leonard was very embarrassed, but he didn't know what to say. As she talked, Leonard thought about an invention he needed. What about a pair of thick earmuffs? If he wore them, he wouldn't be able to hear her. No, that wouldn't work. She'd just talk louder. What about a buzzer? The buzzer could buzz louder when she talked louder. If she wanted the buzzer to stop, she'd have to talk softly.

"Now there's an invention," she said, pointing to something. She and Leonard were in front of a bakery. The window was filled with things that looked so good to eat that Leonard tried not to look at them. Grandmother Esther seemed to be pointing at the door. "Yes, a very simple invention, but a very clever one."

"What invention is that?" Leonard asked.

"The electric eye, of course," she said. Leonard didn't know what she was talking about. "The electric what?" he asked.

"The electric eye. Don't tell me you don't know what an electric eye is."

Before he could respond, she opened the door to the bakery. She pointed to a tiny light that was on one side of the door, about half a meter from the floor. "There it is," she said. "The electric eye."

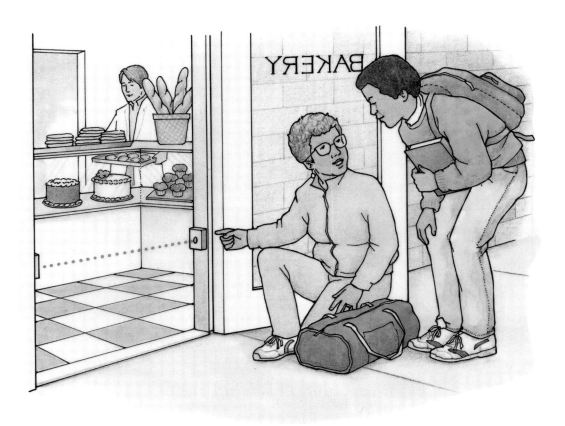

"What does it do?" Leonard asked.

"It tells the shopkeeper that you're coming into the shop. Watch." She held her hand in front of the little beam of light that came from the electric eye. As soon as she did, a buzzer sounded in the back of the bakery. "That's just what happens when you walk into the store." She explained how the electric eye worked. The beam of light went from one side of the door to the other. As long as the beam reached a little target on the other side of the door, nothing happened. But when something got in the way of that beam of light and kept it from reaching the target, the buzzer sounded. She explained that the buzzer kept sounding as long as the beam was broken. So when somebody walked in the door, the body would stop the beam of light from reaching the target. When the body stopped the beam, the buzzer sounded. That buzzer told the shopkeeper that somebody was going through the door.

Grandmother Esther was kneeling in front of the doorway as she explained how the beam worked. Several people were trying to get into the bakery. They waited as she explained the electric eye. The shopkeeper was standing behind the counter, looking at her. When she finished her explanation of the electric eye, she said, "This is a good example of a clever invention. The electric eye is a simple invention, but it has many, many uses."

One of the people who was trying to get into the store said, "Very interesting."

The other person said, "Yes, very interesting."

The shopkeeper said, "Excuse me, could you stand aside and let these people come in?"

Leonard said, "Come on, Grandma, you're blocking the doorway."

And Grandmother Esther said, "Of course, the electric eye is not as great an invention as the airplane or the electric light. But the electric eye serves many needs."

The shopkeeper said, "Yes, it does."

Leonard said, "Come on, Grandma, I've got to go to school."

Number your paper from 1 through 24.

Skill Items

He responded to her clever solution.

1. What word means **reacted**?
2. What word means **very smart**?
3. What word refers to solving a problem?

Review Items

4. Which object is the hottest?
5. What is the temperature of that object?
6. Which object is the coldest?
7. What is the temperature of that object?

A    B    C

20 degrees   60 degrees   35 degrees

8. Let's say you saw a ship far out on the ocean. Would you be able to see the **whole ship** or just the **top part?**
9. Would you see **more** of the ship or **less** of the ship if the world was flat?

10. Who was the first president of the United States?
11. Who is the president of the United States today?
12. Which direction would you go to get from Canada to the main part of the United States?
13. Which country is **larger,** Canada or the United States?
14. Which country is **colder,** Canada or the United States?
15. Where do **more** people live, in Canada or in the United States?

16. What part of the world is shown with the arrows?
17. How far is it from **A** to **B?**
18. How far is it from **C** to **D?**

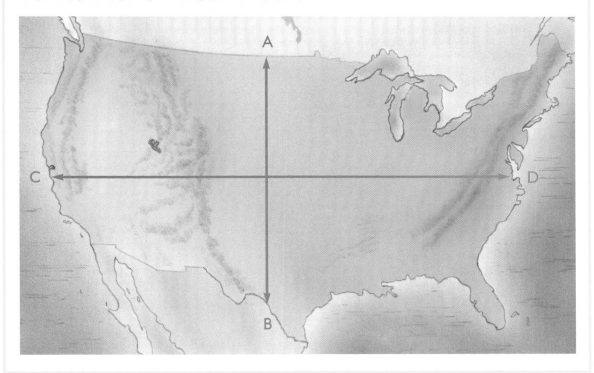

The arrows show that the temperature is going up on thermometer A and going down on thermometer B.

19. In which picture is the water getting colder, **A** or **B?**

20. In which picture is the water getting hotter, **A** or **B?**

A

B

21. What part does **Q** show?

22. What part does **R** show?

23. What part does **S** show?

24. What part does **T** show?

Q

R

S

T

A

1	2	3
1. <u>clear</u>er	1. tone	1. assignment
2. <u>de</u>vice	2. arithmetic	2. drawings
3. <u>supp</u>er	3. stinks	3. enter
4. <u>out</u>fit	4. solution	4. sour
	5. giggled	

B

A Good Idea

The next evening, after supper, it happened. Leonard had no warning that it would happen. But it did. Everything in his mind suddenly came together and he had the idea for a great invention.

Here's how it happened: After supper, he went to his room to get a pencil. He was going to make some more drawings of ideas for inventions. When he started back to the kitchen, Grandmother Esther hollered at him, "Turn off the light in your room. Remember to save energy."

Leonard turned around, went back to his room, turned off the light, and stood there in the dark room. He felt the idea coming into his head. It got bigger and clearer and . . . "Hot dog!" he shouted. He shouted, "What an idea for an invention! Hot dog!"

He ran into the kitchen. "I've got it. What an idea! This

is the best idea anybody ever had for an invention!"

His mother smiled. "I'll bet it's a machine that makes up a list of things you need at the store."

"Stop talking about that stupid machine," Grandmother Esther yelled from the other room. She ran into the kitchen. She was wearing her exercise outfit. Grandmother Esther asked, "What's your idea, Leonard?"

Leonard said, "Let me explain how it's going to work. It's dark outside. And it's dark in the living room of your house. But when you walk through the door to the living room, the light goes on automatically. The light stays on as long as you're in the living room. But when you leave the living room, the light goes off."

Leonard's mother shook her head. "That sounds far too difficult."

Grandmother Esther said, "It sounds difficult to you because you don't know how the electric eye works."

"The electric eye?" Leonard's mother asked.

Leonard said, "Here's how it works, Mom. There's a little beam of light that goes across the doorway to the living room. When you enter the room, you break the beam. When you break that beam, the light turns on. Then when you leave the room, you break the beam and the light goes off."

"Oh, my," Leonard's mother said. He could tell from her tone of voice that she didn't understand what he said.

"Good thinking," Grandmother Esther said, and slapped Leonard on the back. "That's a fine idea for an invention, a fine idea."

"Thank you," Leonard said.

Grandmother Esther made a sour looking face. Slowly she said, "There's one big problem with being a good inventor. You have to think of all the things that could go wrong."

"What could go wrong?" Leonard asked.

Grandmother Esther explained. "When you break the beam one time, the light goes on. When you break the beam the next time, the light goes off. When you break the beam the next time, the light goes on."

"Right," Leonard said.

"That's the problem," Grandmother Esther said. "What if two people walk into a dark room? When the first one goes into the room, the light will go on. Now the second person goes into the room. What happens to the light?"

"It goes off," Leonard said very sadly. He shook his head. "Now both people are in the dark, and my invention stinks."

"Wrong!" Grandmother Esther shouted. "Both people are in the dark, but your invention does not stink. Every invention has problems. An inventor has to look at these problems and try to solve them. But you must remember that inventing something is more than just getting an idea. You must work on that idea until it is a good idea. Then you must take that good idea and make it into a good invention. Just because there's a problem doesn't mean that you give up. You've got a great idea."

Leonard's mother said, "I have a great idea for an invention. It's a machine that . . ."

"Not now," Grandmother Esther said. "We're close to a <u>real</u> invention."

Leonard said, "I'll just have to think about the problem and try to figure out how to solve it."

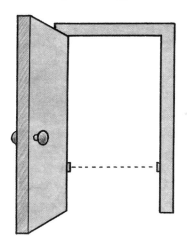
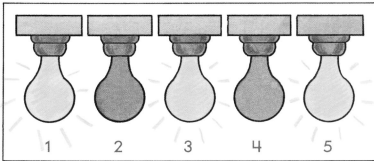

Number your paper from 1 through 26.

Review Items

1. If you go east from Australia, what ocean do you go through?
2. What is a group of kangaroos called?
3. What is a baby kangaroo called?
4. A kangaroo is ▮▮▮ centimeters long when it is born.
5. Big kangaroos grow to be as big as a ▮▮▮.

---

6. The picture shows half a hailstone. How many times did the stone go through a cloud?

---

7. Write the letter of the plane that is in the **warmest** air.
8. Write the letter of the plane that is in the **coldest** air.

	5 miles high
M	4 miles high
L	3 miles high
K	2 miles high
	1 mile high
N	

Here's how an electric eye at a store works.

9. When somebody walks in the door, the body stops the beam of light from reaching the ████.

10. When the body stops the beam, what does the device do next?

11. What does that tell the shopkeeper?

12. Write the letter of the layer that went into the pile first.

13. Write the letter of the layer that went into the pile next.

14. Write the letter of the layer that went into the pile last.

15. Write the letter of the layer that we live in.

16. What's the name of layer C?

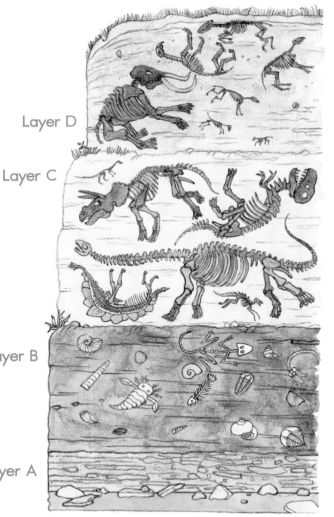

Layer D

Layer C

Layer B

Layer A

17. A mile is a little more than ▮▮▮ feet.

18. Which letter shows where Australia is?
19. Which letter shows where the United States is?
20. Which letter shows where Canada is?
21. Which letter shows where the Pacific Ocean is?

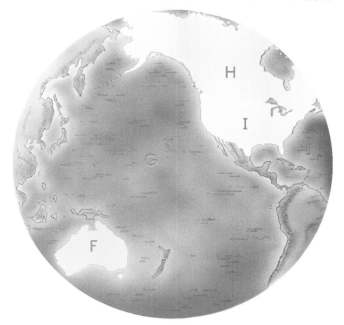

22. Name the country that is just north of the United States.
23. In what country are peacocks wild animals?

Here's how fast different things can go:
- 20 miles per hour
- 200 miles per hour
- 35 miles per hour
- 500 miles per hour

24. Which speed tells how fast a fast man can run?
25. Which speed tells how fast a jet can fly?

A

1	2	3
1. <u>bath</u>room	1. entering	1. shaft
2. <u>one</u>-way	2. drums	2. whether
3. <u>home</u>work	3. practicing	3. drew
4. <u>out</u>fit	4. realizing	4. goose

B ONE WAY

Leonard said to himself, "Figure out how to solve that problem." It was a real problem. Every time the beam is broken, the lights change. If they are on, they go off. So if somebody is in a room with the lights on and somebody else comes into the room, the beam is broken and the lights go off.

He was on his way to school. He walked past the bakery. For a moment he remembered how embarrassed he had been when Grandmother Esther blocked the people who were trying to come into the store.

From time to time his mind would notice other things around him, but most of the time it was busy with the problem. "Think."

Then Leonard realized that he was looking at a sign. "One way," the sign said. And it had an arrow. "One way." Although Leonard didn't figure out the answer to his problem at that moment, he had a very strange feeling, as if he were very close to the answer. Leonard said, "My device has to know which way you are going. It has to know if you are entering the room or leaving the room." Leonard crossed the street. Then he stopped and said out loud, "But one electric eye can't tell whether you're coming in or going out."

Two boys who were walking to school giggled and pointed at Leonard. When Leonard saw them pointing, he realized how crazy he must have looked as he talked to himself.

Later that day in school, Leonard was supposed to be doing his arithmetic homework. He liked arithmetic and he was good at it, but he couldn't seem to work on it that day. He kept thinking of the problem and the one-way sign. Without realizing what he was doing, he drew the sign on his paper.

He studied the arrow. He traced it with his pencil three or four times. Then he traced over the letters in the sign. Then he put two dots next to each other on the shaft of the arrow. Suddenly, he felt goose bumps all over his face and down his back. He almost jumped out of his seat. "Wow!" he shouted. "I've got it!"

Everybody in the class was looking at him. He

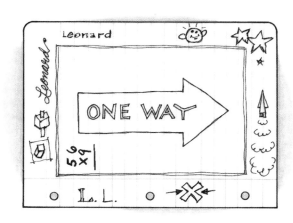

could feel his face becoming very hot. He cleared his throat and coughed. Then he looked down at his paper. He could still feel the eyes of everybody in the room looking at him. Then he heard the teacher's voice. "Is anything wrong, Leonard?"

Leonard looked up. "No, no. I just figured out the solution to a problem I've been working on."

The teacher said, "I'm glad to see that you are so excited about solving your arithmetic problems, but when you work out the solution to the next problem, try to be a little more quiet about it."

•   •   •

After school that day, Leonard ran home. It felt great to run. Sometimes when he ran he felt heavy, but as he went  home that afternoon, he felt very light and very fast. He could feel the wind on his face. He raced with the cars when they started out from stop signs. He could stay with them for more than half a city block.

When he got home, he ran into the house. "Grandma!" he shouted. "I've got it!" Grandmother Esther was practicing on her drums. Leonard's mother was in the hall. She was wearing earmuffs.

Leonard told Grandmother Esther how to solve the problem. "On the side of the door we put two electric eyes, not one." Leonard continued, "The electric eyes are side by side. When somebody goes through the door, they will break one beam first, then the second beam. If the outside beam is broken first and the inside beam is broken next, the person is moving <u>into</u> the room."

Leonard continued to explain, "If the inside beam is broken first and the outside beam is broken next, the person is moving <u>out</u> of the room. We make the electric eye device turn on the light if somebody goes <u>into</u> the room and turn <u>off</u> the light if somebody goes <u>out</u> of the room."

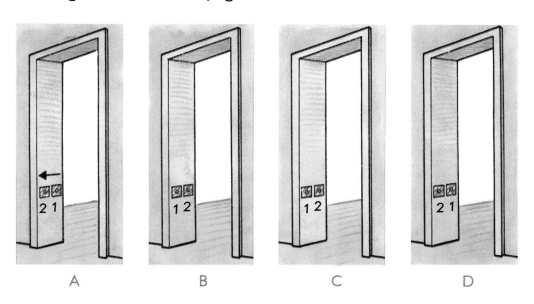

A   B   C   D

C Number your paper from 1 through 27.

Story Items

1. In today's story, what was Leonard doing that made two boys on the street giggle and point at him?
2. What did Leonard do when he figured out the solution?
3. Where was he?
4. When Leonard got home, his mother was wearing earmuffs. Why?
5. How many electric eyes will Leonard use?
6. How many beams will go across the doorway?

7. Leonard's first invention had problems. Let's say two people walk into a dark room. What happens to the light in the room when the first person enters?
8. What happens to the light when the second person enters?

Skill Items

Use the words in the box to write complete sentences.

device	outfit	solution	entered
impressed	mentioned	responded	vocabulary

9. They were ▨ by her large ▨.
10. He ▨ to her clever ▨.

Review Items

11. When a plane flies from New York City to San Francisco, is it flying in the **same direction** or the **opposite direction** as the wind?

Write **W** for warm-blooded animals and **C** for cold-blooded animals.

12. beetle   15. spider
13. cow   16. bee
14. horse

17. Which came **earlier** on Earth, dinosaurs or horses?
18. Which came **earlier** on Earth, strange sea animals or dinosaurs?

19. What are clouds made of?
20. What kind of cloud does the picture show?
21. What happens to a drop at **B**?

22. Lee is 12 miles high. Joan is 6 miles high. Who is colder?
23. Tell why.

24. Write the letters of 3 things that were true of humans 40 thousand years ago.
  - a. They lived in caves.
  - b. They were shorter than people of today.
  - c. They were taller than people of today.
  - d. They wore animal skins.
  - e. They wore hats.
  - f. They rode bikes.
  - g. They drove cars.

25. Write the letter of each thing that was invented after 1800.

a. televisions	e. rafts	i. refrigerators
b. cars	f. trains	j. tape recorders
c. doors	g. bicycles	k. pyramids
d. telephones	h. movies	l. radios

Study Items

Grandmother Esther keeps talking about what a great invention the electric light bulb is. The man who invented it was named Thomas Alva Edison.

26. Find out when he invented the electric light bulb.
27. Find out 2 other things that he invented.

A

1	2
1. diagram	1. secret
2. lawyer	2. rapped
3. purchase	3. shame
4. attorney	4. booming
5. permission	5. snappy
6. electrical	6. sighed

B

Another Problem

"That's a great solution," Grandmother Esther said. Leonard had just explained his idea. Instead of one electric eye on the side of the door, he would make two of them. When somebody walked into the room, the body would break one beam before the other beam. If the outside beam was broken first, the person was moving into the room. If the inside beam was broken first, the person was moving out of the room.

Leonard explained, "As soon as I saw that arrow on the one-way sign, I knew that I was close to the solution."

"Good job," Grandmother Esther said and rapped out a snappy drum roll. Grandmother Esther continued, "But there is still one problem."

"Oh, no," Leonard said. "Not another problem."

Grandmother Esther hit the biggest drum. Then she said, "Your machine can tell whether somebody comes into the room or goes out of the room. And your machine turns off the lights when somebody leaves the room."

Then she said, "But what would happen if three people were sitting in the room reading and one of them left the room?"

Leonard sighed and said, "The light would go off."

Leonard felt dumb for not seeing this problem before his grandmother pointed it out. The electric eye device that he had imagined couldn't count. It couldn't tell if one person was in the room or if ten were in the room. The only thing Leonard's device knew how to do was to turn the lights on if somebody came into the room and turn them off if somebody left the room. But the device didn't know how many people were in the room.

Grandmother Esther said, "Your invention has to know how to count people in the room." Then she made a long drum roll and ended it with a terribly loud boom. "So, make it count," she said.

"How do I do that?" Leonard asked.

☾ She responded, "What if you had a counter on your device? When a person went into the room, the counter would count one. When the next person went into the room, the counter would count again—two. With a counter, your device would know how many people are in the room. It wouldn't shut off the lights until the last person left the room."

For a few moments, Leonard thought about what she said. Then he said, "I get it. The lights wouldn't go off if there were still some people in the room." Then he added, "But I don't know how to make the device count."

"Think, think, think," she said and began to tap on the smallest drum. "Think, Leonard, think," she repeated.

Leonard knew that she wasn't going to tell him any more about how to make the device count, so he left the room and began to think.

For nearly the rest of the day, Leonard's mind kept hearing his grandmother say, "Think, think, think." But the problem was much harder for Leonard than she made it sound. He thought and thought.

Just before supper, he went into the bathroom. He filled the sink with water and washed his hands. When he started to let the water out of the ⭐ sink, he got the idea. The water would keep going out of the sink until the sink was empty. The water kept going out until there was <u>zero</u> water in the sink. That was the secret. "Count to zero," he said out loud.

He ran to his room and got some paper. Then he made a little drawing that showed how the device could count. Look at the drawing that he made.

Leonard ran into the kitchen. Grandmother Esther was starting to eat her salad. He showed her the drawing and explained. "The device can tell each time somebody goes into the room and each time somebody goes out. So we make a counter that counts <u>forward</u> each time somebody goes into the room. If four people go into the room, the counter counts one, two, three, four. Each time somebody leaves the room, the counter counts <u>backward</u>. So if three people leave, the counter counts backward: three, two, one. But the lights don't go off until the counter counts back to zero."

Leonard continued to explain, "When the last person leaves the room, the counter counts back to zero. Now the lights go off."

Grandmother Esther jumped out of her chair, threw her arms around Leonard, and gave him a kiss.

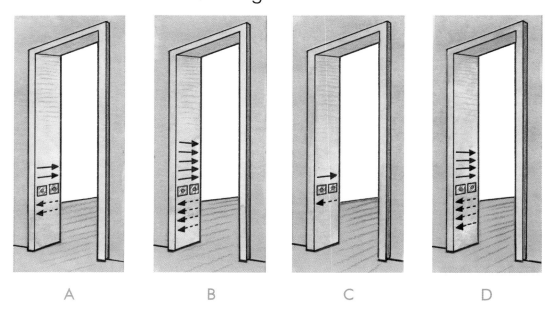

A   B   C   D

Number your paper from 1 through 25.

Story Items

1. How many electric eyes did Leonard use for his invention?
2. How many beams went across the doorway?
3. If a person moves into a room, which beam will be broken first—the inside beam or the outside beam?
4. Which beam will be broken next?

5. The solid arrows show how many times people went into the room. How many people went into the room?
6. The dotted arrows show how many times people left the room. How many people left the room?
7. Are the lights on in the room?
8. How many more people would have to leave the room before the lights go off?

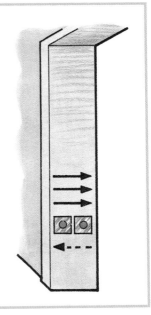

Here are three events that happened in the story.
Write **beginning, middle,** or **end** for each event.

9. The water kept going out until there was zero water in the sink.
10. Leonard told Grandmother Esther that the one-way sign helped him figure out a solution.
11. Leonard told Grandmother Esther how the counter on his device would work.

Review Items

12. When a plane flies from New York City to San Francisco, is it flying in the **same direction** or the **opposite direction** as the wind?

Jar X is filled with ocean water. Jar Y is filled with fresh water.

13. Which jar is heavier?
14. Which jar will freeze at 32 degrees?
15. Will the other jar freeze when it is **more than 32 degrees** or **less than 32 degrees?**

X

Y

Write the time for each event shown on the time line.

16. Eric and Tom were in the city of the future.

17. The year Thrig was from

18. Now

19. You were born.

20. Eric and Tom were in San Francisco.

21. The United States became a country.

22. Columbus discovered America.

23. Eric and Tom were in the Land of the Vikings.

24. Eric and Tom were in Egypt.

25. Eric and Tom saw a saber-toothed tiger.

A

1	2
1. business	1. model
2. manufacturer	2. patent
3. disappointed	3. purchase
4. flood	4. supply
5. turner-off-er	5. automatic

3	4
1. company	1. owe
2. connected	2. attorney
3. diagrams	3. electrical
4. lawyers	4. permission

B

Leonard's Model

It's easy to say that the invention will count things, but it's a much harder job to build a device that counts. Grandmother Esther was a big help for this part of the job. She knew a lot about electricity. Grandmother Esther got books for Leonard that showed him where to buy electric eyes and how to hook electric wires up to make the electric eyes work. These books also showed where to purchase electric counters. After Leonard and his grandmother decided which type of electric eyes they wanted, she made a few phone calls, took Leonard with her in her jeep, and bought the supplies that they needed to build the model.

"Now remember, Leonard," she said as they left the electrical supply store. "You owe me sixty dollars. When you start making money from your invention, just remember that I'm giving up my fishing trip so that you can build your invention."

"You shouldn't give up your fishing trip, Grandmother," he said. "I'll get the money . . . ."

"I'm kidding you," she said. "I'd much rather invent something than go fishing any time." She started up the jeep and made the engine roar loudly. Suddenly, the jeep jumped forward, snapping Leonard's head back. And off they went to their home.

Leonard and his grandmother built a model of the electric eye device. The model was a little doorway that was about one meter tall. There was a light bulb connected to the top of the doorway.

To show how the model worked, Leonard used a large teddy bear and large dolls. Leonard moved these objects through the doorway. An object would break the outside beam first, then the inside beam. As soon as the first object broke both beams, the light went on. Leonard would move more objects through the doorway and the light would stay on.

Then Leonard would begin to move the objects the other way. The light would stay on until the last object went back through the doorway. Then the light would go off.

"This device works!" Leonard shouted after he and his grandmother had tested it four times. "It works. We've invented an automatic light turner-off-er!"

But Leonard's work was not finished. He had a model of the invention, and that model worked. But now he had to protect his invention. An invention needs protection from people who copy it and say that it is their invention. To protect an invention, the inventor gets a patent. When an invention is patented, the only person who can make copies of that invention is the inventor. If other people want to make copies of it, they have to get permission from the inventor. The inventor may tell somebody that it is all right to make copies of the invention. But the inventor doesn't usually <u>give</u> somebody this right. The inventor <u>sells</u> the right. The inventor may say this to the person who wants to make copies: "Each time you make a copy, you must give me so much money." Maybe the person has to pay five dollars for each copy ✦ that is built. Maybe the inventor sells the whole patent to a company that wants to make copies of the invention. If the invention is good, the inventor may make a lot of money from that invention.

But the first step is to get a patent. Without a patent, the inventor has no protection against people who want to make copies of the invention. Getting a patent is very difficult. There are special lawyers who do nothing but get patents for inventors. These lawyers are called patent attorneys. Grandmother Esther explained patents and patent attorneys to Leonard. Then she phoned a patent attorney and told the attorney that Leonard wanted to patent his invention.

Leonard and his grandmother had three meetings with the patent attorney. The attorney answered hundreds of questions. Leonard and Grandmother Esther made diagrams of the invention for her.

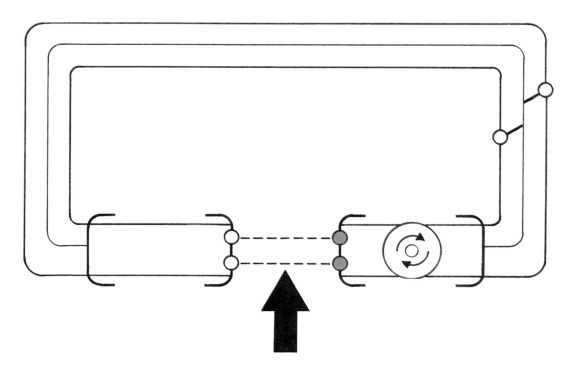

When they finally finished their meetings with the patent attorney, Grandmother Esther said, "Now you owe me another three thousand dollars. If your invention doesn't start making some money, I'll have to give up my flying lessons."

"You're great, Grandma," Leonard said. "You're just great."

"Oh, stop it," Grandmother Esther said and slapped Leonard on the back.

C Number your paper from 1 through 22.

Skill Items

The patent attorney wrote an agreement.

1. What do we call a lawyer whose special job is getting patents for new inventions?
2. What word means **lawyer?**
3. What word means a **promise made by people?**
4. What word names a license for somebody to be the only person who can make a product?

Review Items

5. The solid arrows show how many times people went into the room. How many people went into the room?
6. The dotted arrows show how many times people left the room. How many people left the room?
7. Are the lights on in the room?
8. How many more people would have to leave the room before the lights go off?

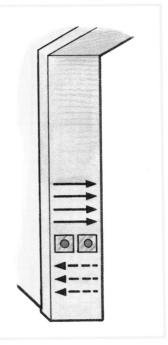

Answer these questions about the counter on Leonard's device:

9. Every time somebody goes into the room, what does the counter do?
   - + 1   - – 1   - – 0
10. Every time somebody goes out of the room, what does the counter do?
    - + 1   - – 1   - – 0
11. What number does the counter end up at when the last person leaves the room?
12. What happens to the lights when the counter gets to that number?

13. Write **A, B, C,** and **D** on your paper. For each picture, tell if the lights in the room are on or off. The solid arrows show people going into the room. The dotted arrows show people leaving the room.

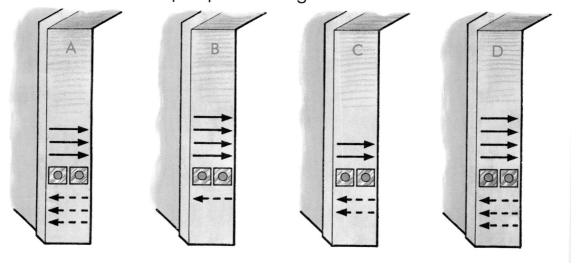

14. Two things happen to melted rock when it moves down the sides of a volcano. Name those 2 things.
15. What is it called when the earth shakes and cracks?
16. How many seconds are in one minute?
17. How many legs does an insect have?
18. How many legs does a fly have?
19. How many legs does a bee have?
20. How many legs does a spider have?
21. How many parts does a spider's body have?
22. How many parts does a fly's body have?

TEST 10

Number your paper from 1 through 36.

1. The men who invented the first airplane saw a need. What need?

Here's how an electric eye works.

2. When somebody walks in the door of the store, the body stops the beam of light from reaching the ▬▬.
3. When the body stops the beam, what does the device do next?
4. What does that tell the shopkeeper?

Here's the rule about an electric eye: **Each time the beam of light is broken, the light changes.**

5. The light is off. The beam is broken 2 times. Is the light **on** or **off** at the end?
6. The light is off. The beam is broken 5 times. Is the light **on** or **off** at the end?
7. The light is off. The beam is broken 8 times. Is the light **on** or **off** at the end?

8. How many electric eyes did Leonard use?
9. How many beams went across the doorway?
10. If a person moves **into** a room, which beam will be broken first—the inside beam or the outside beam?
11. Which beam will be broken next?

The picture shows two electric eye beams on the side of doors. The number **1** shows the beam that is broken first. The number **2** shows the beam that is broken next. Write the letter of the correct arrow for each doorway.

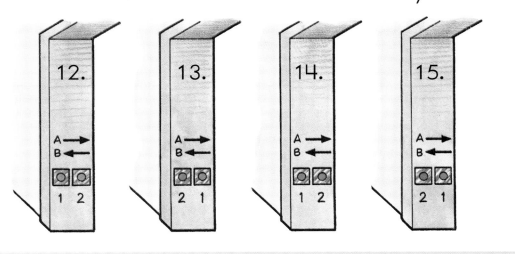

Answer these questions about the counter on Leonard's device:

16. Every time somebody goes into the room, what does the counter do?

    • + 1   • – 1   • + 0

17. Every time somebody goes out of the room, what does the counter do?

    • + 1   • – 1   • + 0

18. What number does the counter end up at when the last person leaves the room?

19. What happens to the lights when the counter gets to that number?

20. The solid arrows show how many times people went into the room. How many people went into the room?
21. The dotted arrows show how many times people left the room. How many people left the room?
22. Are the lights on in the room?
23. How many more people would have to leave the room before the lights go off?

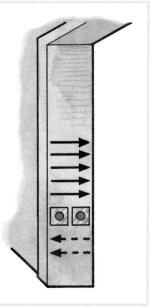

For each picture, tell if the lights in the room are **on** or **off**. The solid arrows show people going into the room. The dotted arrows show people leaving the room.

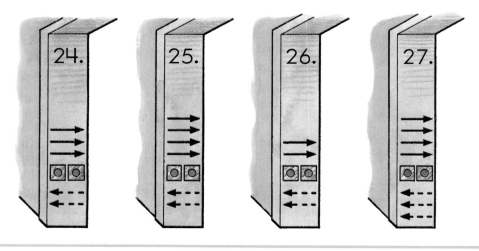

28. What does an inventor get to protect an invention?
29. Special lawyers who get protection for inventions are called .

For each item, write the underlined word from the sentences in the box.

> She <u>automatically</u> <u>arranged</u> the flowers.
> They were <u>impressed</u> by her large <u>vocabulary</u>.
> He <u>responded</u> to her <u>clever</u> <u>solution</u>.

30. What underlining means **reacted**?
31. What underlining means that she put things where she wanted them?
32. What underlining refers to all the words a person knows?
33. What underlining means they thought her vocabulary was very good?
34. What underlining means **very smart**?
35. What underlining means **without thinking**?
36. What underlining refers to solving a problem?

=== END OF TEST 10 ===

Fact Game Answer Key

Lesson 60

2. 1868, 1796, 1996

3. 2100, 2010, 2222

4. yards,
   feet,
   centimeters

5. days,
   hours,
   weeks

6. inches per minute,
   meters per week,
   feet per second

7. A. 4 thousand years in
      the future
   B. 2400
   C. *

8. D. *
   E. 1906
   F. 1776

9. G. 3 thousand years
      ago

H. 5 thousand years
   ago

 I. 40 thousand years
   ago

10. A. Egypt
    B. Italy
    C. Spain

11. D. Turkey
    E. Greece

12. Texas, New York City,
    Concord

Lesson 70

2. a. 10 feet
   b. 3 centimeters

3. A. United States
   B. Pacific Ocean

4. C. Canada
   D. Australia

5. A. Mexico
   B. San Francisco
   C. Canada

6. D. United States
   E. Concord
   F. Spain

7. G. Land of the Vikings
   H. Italy
   I. Greece

8. J. Egypt
   K. Turkey

9. A. 4 thousand years in the future
   B. 2400
   C. correct answer

10. D. correct answer
    E. 1906
    F. 1777

11. G. 1776
    H. 1492
    I. 1000

12. J. 3 thousand years ago
    K. 5 thousand years ago
    L. 40 thousand years ago

Lesson 80

2. A. Canada
   B. United States

3. 60

4. a. Canada
   b. Canada
   c. United States

5. a. C
   b. D

6. a. A
   b. B
   c. D

7. a. D
   b. Mesozoic

8. a. A
   b. D
   c. C

9. A. Triceratops
   B. Tyrannosaurus

10. a. dinosaurs
    b. earlier

11. a. drops of water
    b. storm clouds

12. a. A
    b. B

2. a. Canada
   b. United States

3. a. United States
   b. Canada

4. A. Tyrannosaurus
   B. Triceratops

5. 60

6. a. B
   b. C

7. It cools and gets hard.

8. a. R
   b. S

9. earthquake

10. a. inventor
    b. invention

11. 6

12. earlier

Lesson 100

2. a. problems; needs
   b. invent

3. A $\longrightarrow$ B $\longleftarrow$ C $\longrightarrow$ D $\longleftarrow$

4. to get places faster; to use shorter routes

5. a. off
   b. on

6. a. zero
   b. They turn off.

7. a. counts forward; plusses one
   b. counts backward; minuses one

8. a. outside beam
   b. inside beam
   c. on

9. A. on   C. off
   B. off   D. on

10. a. into the room
    b. out of the room

11. a. 2
    b. 2

12. a. patent
    b. patent attorneys

VOCABULARY SENTENCES

1. A beagle exercises at a health spa.

2. You measure your weight in pounds.

3. The dog was healthy compared to the rat.

4. They waded into the stream to remove tadpoles.

5. The fly boasted about escaping from the spider.

6. The workers propped up the cage with steel bars.

7. Hunters were stationed at the opposite ends of the field.

8. He motioned to the flight attendant ahead of him.

9. The traffic was moving forty miles per hour.

10. He is supposed to make a decision in a couple of days.

11. Several paths continued for a great distance.

12. Boiling water will thaw ice in a few moments.

13. They were eager to hear the announcement.

14. The lifeboat disappeared in the whirlpool.

15. The smoke swirled in enormous billows.

16. The occasional foul smell was normal.

17. They constructed an enormous machine.

18. She survived until she was rescued.

19. The palace guards spoke different languages.

20. His argument convinced them to buy an appliance.

21. The army was soundly defeated near the village.

22. Police officers checked the ship's cargo.

23. She paid the correct amount.

24. The champions performed perfectly.

25. The smell attracted flies immediately.

26. The rim of the volcano exploded.

27. The new exhibit displayed mysterious fish.

28. She automatically arranged the flowers.

29. They were impressed by her large vocabulary.

30. He responded to her clever solution.

31. The patent attorney wrote an agreement.